Success
is in
Giving

Success is in Giving

WESLEY HARRIS

Wrightbooks

BY THE SAME AUTHOR:

Battlelines
*Nice Guys Can Win!
*You've Got What It Takes
*Truth Stranger Than Fiction

*Published by and available from Wrightbooks

Wrightbooks Pty Ltd
PO Box 270
Elsternwick
Victoria 3185
Ph: (03) 9532 7082
Fax: (03) 9532 7084
Email: wbooks@ozemail.com.au

National Library of Australia Cataloguing-in-publication data:

Harris, Wesley, 1928-.
Success is in giving.
ISBN 1 875857 71 0.
1. Generosity. 2. Gifts. 3. Success. I. Title.
179.9

Cover design by Rob Cowpe
Printed in Australia by McPhersons Printing Group

ISBN: 1 875857 71 0

*This book is dedicated
to my brother Railton
who gave
a lifetime of selfless service
and shunned any recognition or thanks*

Contents

Contents (Cont'd)

Preface

According to scientist Sir James Dewar, minds are like parachutes; they only function when they are open. This book is for those with minds capable of opening to some new thoughts on old subjects – like how to be successful, for example.

Success may mean making lots of money, achieving academic success, gaining political power or finding fame. These are among the stereotypes of success, and fair enough. But in achieving them, the means employed will affect the quality of the 'success' enjoyed.

Going for gold may be fine. Dreaming of the different lifestyle which could come with riches honestly gained is quite legitimate and there are modern Dick Whittingtons for whom the dream has come true. Good for them! The dream of making a million – or more – may be fair enough and just what some people need to kindle the fires of enthusiasm. But riches alone may not be indicative of true 'success'. The measure of a man or woman may be in what they *give* more than in what they *get*.

The miser in his mouldy mansion may have pots of money but if in the process of accumulating it he has cut himself off from friendship and allowed the milk of human kindness to become curdled, what price his 'success'? The same sort of thing could be said about achievements in the academic or political fields.

However, there are many stories of people who, in the best sense, have helped themselves and helped lots of other people as well. They haven't risen by putting others down but by teaching them how to lift themselves up. They have got what they wanted through helping other people get what they wanted; their dream has been realised in and through helping others to discover theirs.

My contention is that any recipe for success should include the ingredient of giving, otherwise life is likely to go flat. Helping other people to succeed may be the best way to succeed ourselves. But just as success may take many forms, so also may giving.

In this book I not only write about giving money but also about giving time, dreams, loyalty, happiness and much else. A secret of living successfully is being ready to give something of what we *are* as well as of what we've *got*. Emerson said that rings and jewels are only apologies for gifts, the true gift is the gift of ourselves.

There is a legend about a man journeying in the mountains who found a precious stone in a stream. The following day he met another traveller who was hungry and had no food, so he offered to share his provisions. When he opened his bag the hungry traveller saw the jewel, admired it, and wanted it. He asked if he could have it, and the wanderer was happy to give it to him.

The traveller continued on his way, rejoicing in the fact that he could sell the jewel for enough money to keep him content for life. But a few days later he retraced his steps, seeking his benefactor. When he found him he gave him back the stone, saying, "I have been thinking, and I want to return your jewel to you. I know how valuable it is, but I give it back to you in the hope that you can give me something much more precious. If you can, give me what you have within you that enabled you to give me the stone."

The giving spirit is itself a gift to be desired and the key to true success. Trust me!

Wesley Harris
Melbourne, May 1998

~ 1 ~

How to Give

> It's not what you do but the
> way that you do it.
>
> Popular song

*T*his book might have been called: *Successful people know*
what *to give*. That would have been to make a valid and a vital
point which is reiterated frequently in the following chapters.
However, it is also important to recognise the importance of
knowing *how* to give.

A husband might buy a bunch of flowers and fling them across
the room at his wife. Would they still be appreciated despite the
manner of their delivery? Well, they might be but I know some
wives who would probably say, "Not likely!" *How* we give may be
as expressive as what we give for there is more to giving than
delivering goods and services. Giving is an art.

It is possible to patronise or pauperise people by our giving.
Unwittingly perhaps, we can take away independence or a sense
of self-worth and actually leave people feeling poorer because of
our gift.

Some people make a practice of giving presents which appeal
to *them* on the assumption that they will therefore be appealing to

the recipient. But this may not follow. The better way is to make a study of the needs and tastes of the other person and then give accordingly.

What holds good for individuals may also pertain to companies. For example, being 'user friendly' is vital for those who would survive in an increasingly competitive market. To ensure continuing success there is need for constant evaluation of customer reaction. The windows of the boardroom must be open to the wind-like currents of opinion in the outside world.

Sufficient Insurance?

It has to be asked whether the strength of appreciation for services rendered is sufficient insurance against any tendency to take business elsewhere. Are customers being given what they really want and not merely what the firm finds it convenient to provide? Successful firms take no chances on such points. They know that it is not only what you do but the way in which you do it that can make all the difference. Customers are not to be taken for granted.

Firms also need to take care in their giving to their staff. It is possible to be very ham-fisted even when giving out 'goodies'. I have heard of firms going ahead with the provision of better staff facilities without bothering to consult those who would use them. In consequence there has been provision for which there was no felt need and a failure to meet needs that were felt. The action may have been well-meaning and the aim an improvement in morale but sometimes the way in which things have been done has almost guaranteed less than wholehearted acceptance.

Clearly, it is possible even to do the right thing and yet do it in the wrong way so that the best of efforts is unappreciated. Successful giving may not be as simple as it sounds. Having had some experience with government aid to third world countries I know that massive assistance does not guarantee commensurate appreciation or goodwill. Some wealthy donating countries are not loved by those they have helped. Is that because of crass ingratitude or because of insensitive benevolence? Sometimes it may have been a bit of both. Certainly, throwing money at problems is not always the answer – although, of course, in some situations nothing else will do if there is insufficient funding.

It may be recognised that overseas aid should never be a substitute for self-help but rather be a stimulus for it. Further, a gift should not be something likely to become an additional burden in time. A prestigious gift for a capital project may become a millstone unless there are ongoing ways and means of maintaining work.

In one third world country I saw a hospital bearing a plaque indicating that it had been the multi-million dollar gift of a certain first world nation. Unfortunately, the building was run down and the work hindered because apparently, the means to maintain it was not forthcoming locally or from overseas. So it is necessary to be thoughtful as well as sensitive in giving. It is said that God is generous with his gifts but economical also. We can take the point for ourselves. Giving should be purposeful not wasteful.

True giving should be an affair of the heart and the head. It is tied up with relationships and they always need to be handled with care. Successful givers are 'people people'; they not only see the dollar signs but the human signs as well. And in my book, theirs are the real success stories.

Check-up

When we buy a car – be it a new Ford or a second-hand Mercedes – we realise that it should be serviced every 10,000 kilometres or the like, whether anything seems to be wrong or not. It simply isn't smart to run a vehicle without making sure that there is water in the cooling system and oil in the engine. The driver with any brains doesn't delay checking until he hears strange clanking sounds or sees steam billowing from beneath the bonnet.

So also with relationships, be they personal, professional, commercial or whatever. They need to be looked after and kept well-serviced. If relationships are good the giving will be good, whatever form it may take. And when it comes to giving, the personal touch will make all the difference. Insensitive benevolence can be an embarrassment. Successful giving helps people to help themselves and grow in the process. Good giving enriches the giver as much and even more than the recipient. In fact, when we know how to give everybody gains; there are no losers.

James Russell Lowell expressed a divine thought in the following words:

> *Not what we give, but what we share,*
> *For the gift without the giver is bare.*
> *Who gives himself with his alms feeds three –*
> *Himself, his hungering neighbour and Me.*

~ 2 ~

Share a Dream

> *A man's reach should exceed his grasp or what's a heaven for?*
> Robert Browning

Walt Disney said of the enterprise which bears his name, "If you can dream it you can do it. This whole thing was started by a mouse". It is certain that if we *don't* dream we'll never do. And that may be the problem with many people; they never dream or they have allowed someone to steal their dreams from them. They have little ambition and muddle on with no specific goals, but *human beings were meant to dream and to share their dreams and the fruit of them with others.*

To give someone a dream may be to change their lives. What is better than to share our vision and inspire someone else to lift their sights and take in wider horizons? It makes the blood flow quicker to hear a recording of the late Martin Luther King declaiming: "I have a dream that one day men will rise up and see that they are made to live together as brothers..." He, although dead, still speaks and shares his vision.

So what's *our* dream and is it worth sharing?

In 1953 graduates from Yale University were asked whether they had clear and specific goals written down with plans for achieving them. Only 3 per cent had. Twenty years later, in 1973, the researchers interviewed the surviving members of the class and discovered that the 3 per cent with specific, written goals were worth more financially than the remaining 97 per cent put together. Other indicators were less easily quantified but in matters such as happiness, fulfilment and being able to help others the 3 per cent also seemed to have fared best.

Some of us may have a broad streak of pessimism in our nature. In talking to ourselves or to others we may easily lapse into the vocabulary of failure and defeat. We may settle for the status quo and convince ourselves that nothing more may be expected. But there is a cure and with faith we can find it. Centuries ago the Hebrew prophet Joel said, "Your young men shall see visions and your old men shall dream dreams". So it is possible to have visions or dreams regardless of age. In the same passage it is claimed that neither nationality nor gender nor social standing need be a barrier or hold people back from the fulfilling life which is their heritage. So *let's go for it* – for our own sake and for the sake of others we may help.

Kick Start

To kick start our confidence we might focus on some of our achievements in the past, some ways in which we have overcome problems and deserved approval. Instead of moping over our failures – and we have all had some – we should aim at building on our successes – and we have all had those also.

Then we might take as our models those who are achievers, people with 'runs on the board'! If we can spend time with such people, so much the better. We need to know what makes them tick, the way they think and the way in which they approach challenges. The temptation may be to take our cues from those who have failed and not even try to 'go for gold' – whatever that means for us. But that is a road which leads nowhere. It is far better to brace up and branch out!

As a young man I was challenged to embark on a particular project when I heard that an old friend had succeeded with something similar. I thought, "If he can do it so can I – and even go one better!" I shared his dream; it came true and the results remain today.

Success stories on a large scale can still be found and if we are made of the right material they will stimulate rather than daunt us. Take the case of Craig and Anna Dean, two people I have met who live in Melbourne. They were married at 19 when Craig was in the Air Force. At the end of his term in the services they were stony broke. Craig worked in the computer industry and put in longer and longer hours in order to make ends meet but his ambition was to have the time to train as a triathlete which was his real interest.

His dream was to be able to afford to spend time doing what he really wanted to do. Still in his twenties, he became involved in home marketing and built a business which has made him a multi-millionaire while still a young man and freed him to follow his special interests.

He and Anna sport a Rolls Royce car. They have a beautiful home and can afford exotic holidays. But their great joy is in the fact that they have been able to help many other people to be fulfilled. They have discovered that one way to get what you want is to help other people get what they want. It is not just that their bank balance has grown; they themselves have grown as people and can now address and inspire large audiences in Australia and in other countries as they *share their dream.*

A Few Rules

In his book *Unlimited Power* Anthony Robbins lays down five rules for those who would dream dreams and then set goals in order to make the dreams come true:

1. ***State your outcome in positive terms.*** *Say what you want to happen. Too often people state what they don't want to happen as their goals.*

2. ***Be as specific as possible***. *How does your outcome look, sound, feel, smell? Also be certain to set a specific completion date and/or term.*

3. ***Have an evidence procedure***. *If you don't know how you'll know when you've achieved your goal, you may already have it. You can be winning and feel like you're losing if you don't keep score.*

4. ***Be in control***. *Your outcome must be initiated and maintained by you. It must not be dependent upon other people having to change themselves for you to be happy. Make sure your outcome reflects things that you can affect directly.*

5. ***Verify that your outcome is ecologically sound and desirable***. *Project into the future the consequences of your actual goal. Your outcome must be one that benefits you and other people.*

I would pick up the last point and emphasise that worthy aims should not only benefit us but others as well. If there's only room for me in my dream then that dream is too small. Dreams are more likely to be achieved if they are shared, for 'mutualism' may be the stuff of which they are made. We can help other people build their dreams and they can help us build ours. What is more, shared dreams can help us grow rather than shrink and shrivel in selfishness. We become great through helping to make other people great.

To dream about *getting* may be legitimate but to dream about *giving* may actually prove more fruitful. On a boat trip to the Great Barrier Reef I talked with an American retiree who was 'living his dream'. He was travelling with his wife, children and grandchildren and he told me how, after finishing military service, he had gone into the construction business and made his millions. However, he confessed that his greatest satisfaction was in his family and his great joy was being able to enlarge their horizons through financing family holidays together in various parts of the world which they wanted to visit.

For other people the shared dream may take a different form. Their desire may be to help their church or favourite charity reach out to people in need. I have a very wealthy friend who has that kind of dream. His greatest joy has not been in making money but in giving it away and being personally identified with people who are impoverished in one way or another. Strangely enough, I have met some miserable millionaires but he would be one of the happiest.

Making Dreams Come True

Of course, we must not only have a dream but set about building it if we and others are to benefit. In a society obsessed with the 'something for nothing syndrome' many look to Lady Luck to make their dreams come true. The 'temples' of the goddess of chance dominate some city skylines but often their precincts are littered with broken dreams and shattered hopes.

Unpopular as the truth may be, the surer route to real success is the way of work and attempting to meet the needs of others through our business or profession or voluntary service. It has been said that to build castles in the air is fine for that is where they ought to be. But underneath the castles we must build solid, down-to-earth foundations and that is likely to entail hard work as is stressed elsewhere in this book. If we keep the dream the work will not feel like drudgery. We will be stimulated by a divine discontent with the status quo and a determination to make things better for everybody.

In the musical play based on Cervantes' *Man of La Mancha* (by Dale Wasserman, lyrics by Joe Darion, music by Mitch Leigh) Don Quixote is considered mad but responds to his critics in the following terms:

> *When life itself seems lunatic, who knows where madness lies? Perhaps to be too practical is madness. To surrender dreams this may be madness. To seek treasure where there is only trash. Too much sanity*

9

*may be madness. And maddest of all, to see life as it is
and not as it should be.*

From the same musical comes the popular song which
includes the following lines:

> *To dream the impossible dream,*
> *To fight the unbeatable foe,*
> *To bear with unbearable sorrow,*
> *To run where the brave dare not go.*
> *To right the unrightable wrong...*
>
> *...And the world will be better for this,*
> *That one man, scorned and covered with scars,*
> *Still strove with his last ounce of courage,*
> *To reach the unreachable stars!*

~ 3 ~

Little Things Can Mean a Lot

> *I come in the little things, saith the Lord.*
>
> Evelyn Underhill

*T*he contention in this book is that as we learn to give we learn to live and that real success in relationships and business, as in other respects, may well depend upon this. But it would be a mistake to imagine that only what appears to us as a big deal will be significant to other people. The big importance of some little things should not be underestimated. What seems inconsequential to us may be very meaningful indeed to somebody else.

A representative of a charitable organisation took a personal interest in an old man sick and alone in a country far from his own. He could not have guessed that his actions could so affect the man that, as a legacy to the charity, he left a farm on the other side of the world now worth several million dollars. The same kind of thing can happen in the context of business. One good turn not only deserves another but can lead to some profitable custom – not that that should be the main motive for showing kindness.

Someone with whom I am acquainted was involved in public work in a town and then moved away. Returning to the place he met a woman who thanked him profusely for what he had done.

He wondered which of his public achievements had earned her appreciation and was 'floored' when she said, "You lit my fire for me". Apparently, she had been sick when he called at her home and, seeking to be helpful, put a match to her fire. And it was that small gesture which had impressed her.

A married woman I knew was collecting in a street for charity. A scruffy little boy stood watching her – until she smiled at him, whereupon he disappeared around a corner only to appear a few minutes later with another boy who was, if anything, more scruffy than himself. "Excuse me, miss," he said, "but would you smile at 'im the same as 'ow you smiled at me?"

One can only speculate about the possible deprivation of those lads which made a smile of such importance. But simple gestures of friendliness may also be significant for a lot of other folk.

More people live closer to more people than ever before as the human ant-heaps we call cities tend to get larger and larger. Yet paradoxically, more people tend to feel isolated, cut off from human contact despite the sea of humanity swirling around them. This struck me one day when I was caught up in the rush hour in central London. I wrote and published a poem which contained the following lines:

> *A thousand secret worlds of destiny and dust*
> *Crammed into a tube train orbiting the inner circle!*
> *Journeying together – yet going different ways;*
> *So near and yet so far.*

London is probably not very different from other large cities in this respect but as a daily commuter there I found that it was possible to sit within centimetres of the same bowler-hatted gent day after day without receiving a flicker of recognition. Many fellow travellers seemed as entrenched behind their newspapers as people used to be behind the iron curtain – well, almost!

A similar depersonalisation can take place in the realm of business causing people to feel that although, with or without their knowledge, their names may be on many computer files there are few people to whom they are important as persons. For that reason we need to take every opportunity of helping to humanise society.

And sometimes even small gestures can make a difference in all sorts of ways.

Be Sensitive

Of course, we must be sensitive enough to respect other people's 'personal space' and the privacy which is everyone's birthright. At least some account must be taken of social conventions and the reserve more characteristic of people of some nationalities than others.

Then sadly, the presence of those disposed to crime in a community may make people understandably cautious of strangers. Those of us who have been in the habit of giving a cheery wave and saying "Hi" to kids playing on the street should not be too surprised at an occasional lack of response. In a sick society kids are quite properly warned of dangers afoot and that for their own good.

But God forbid that a smile, a friendly greeting or a good turn should be regarded as off limits as a general rule. After all, everybody needs the warmth of genuine human contact and that can be expressed by body language if not always in words or deeds.

Of course, some more than others find it easy to reach out to people. My wife's stepfather was a retiree living in the somewhat sedate seaside town of Eastbourne in the United Kingdom. With his engaging grin and the twinkle in his eye he exuded friendliness and had no difficulty in striking up a conversation with tourists or locals alike. Walking with him along the seafront one might have wondered whether there was anyone he didn't know – or want to know. But the extent of what he had contributed to the community by his friendliness and practical help could be gauged when, at his funeral, the congregation which packed a large church included all kinds of people who were his friends – civic leaders and the road sweeper, academics and the intellectually challenged.

We may not all have his kind of temperament but in ways suited to our natures we can give indications of friendliness. Sometimes response may not be immediate but determined goodwill usually wins in the end. It has become a cliché that strangers are friends we have not met before but there is a lot of truth in the saying for all that.

I confess that I am not the kind of husband who normally relishes shopping expeditions with his partner, but setting up home in Melbourne has entailed quite a number of expeditions to department stores and other commercial premises. In some places it has been hard to find an assistant in sight but in others there have been those ready to go out of their way, not only in order to make a sale but to reach out to us as persons. In the best sense of the term they have been 'user friendly' and worth their weight in gold socially and commercially. While aware of the need to watch overheads and staff levels I must say that stores with genuinely helpful employees would be more likely to get my custom!

A smile as an expression of human warmth may cost little but be worth a lot. A warm handshake can convey a great deal. The body language of a genuine 'people person' can speak volumes. And the little things which can help to make a success of community living are things which the poorest of us can afford to give! We don't have to be a billionaire or have the brain of a rocket scientist in order to have something worthwhile to contribute; we've all got what it takes!

~ 4 ~

Character Counts

> *Be more concerned with your character than with your reputation because your character is what you really are while your reputation is merely what others think you are.*
>
> John Wooden

A report in Melbourne's *Herald Sun* dated 11 August 1997 included the following paragraphs:

Gulf War hero Norman Schwarzkopf says character weakness is why many world leaders have failed. He told...business people in Melbourne yesterday that strength of character was the most important ingredient of leadership.

"You'll find about 99% of all the leadership failures in the past 100 years were not failures in talent; they were failures in integrity. The challenge of leadership was to make people want to perform tasks they would not ordinarily do but often this did not happen. A poll in the United States had found 75% of workers lied to their boss.

"When they were asked why they lied to their bosses, they said, 'Because our bosses are unethical and if they

*are unethical then there is no requirement for us to be
ethical.'" General Schwarzkopf said. "It's frightening!"*

Was 'Stormin' Norman' right to place his main emphasis on
the importance of character? I believe that he was. No 'success'
without integrity will be worth having and nothing we give will be
more important than the gift of ourselves. What we *are* will count
for more than anything else. It has been said that "if we sow an act
we will reap a habit; if we sow a habit we will reap a character; if
we sow a character we will reap a destiny".

In that case, what are we to make of lowered standards of
integrity, not least in public life where some have come to regard lies
as the legitimate tools of their trade? If men in authority cheat on
their wives will it be surprising if we wonder whether they may also
cheat on the public? If they appear to be 'feathering their own nest'
in unethical ways is it surprising if cynicism is engendered? Hardly!

On the assumption that influence flows downhill can we be
surprised if people generally and young people in particular take
their cues from those in positions of leadership who fail to give the
right kind of lead? Thomas Jefferson said, "God grant that men of
principle will be our principal men".

The Great Wall of China has been described as 'the largest
fortification ever built'. Dating from the 4th century BC it was
substantially rebuilt in the 15th and 16th centuries. The purpose of
the wall was to defend China from attack from the north. It was
believed that with an average height of about eight metres and a
thickness of between three and four metres no enemy would be able
to penetrate it. However, I have read that in fact some invaders did
get through, not by breaching the wall but by bribing gatekeepers.
Clearly, fortifications without integrity will count for little.

Motives

A cartoon served to illustrate that we may sometimes have reason
to question other people's motives. It depicted some hogs
assembled for feeding with the farmer filling their trough to the

brim. One hog turned to the rest and asked, "Have you ever wondered *why* he is being so good to us?"

Sometimes we encounter people with ulterior motives. They may pretend that they want to give something to us but their real preoccupation is with their own advantage even if it is unfair to us.

On the other hand we know instinctively that we can trust some people. They are open and above board. There are no dark holes or corners in their characters. They are the kind of people with whom we would prefer to do business. And on the basis of the golden rule of doing to others as we would like them to do to us, they are the kind of people we should seek to emulate.

Apart from being right and good in itself, integrity will often prove to be good for business. If people know that they can trust us they will be more likely to give us their patronage. If they know that we are the kind of people who keep promises they will be more ready to recommend us. Our reputation goes before us. People get a kind of 'identikit' picture of the sort of people we are, gathering the details from various sources. Reputation is important – but character is even more important.

It has rightly been said that reputation is what people think we are but character is what we really are. In these days of mass communication there are so-called 'personalities' who are the product of image-makers and in some cases they turn out to be men of straw or cardboard cut-outs rather than real people. On the other hand, as I have discovered, there are some who are in the public eye who are all the better for knowing; the reality is even better than the image.

A good character is made by a succession of thoughts, decisions and actions. It doesn't suddenly come into being in a crisis although it may well be revealed in a time of testing. Life can be like a vice. At times it may squeeze us then whatever is inside will be found out. Thomas Macauley was the English essayist and historian who sacrificed a political career in order to write a monumental *History of England* but who died before its completion. He wrote, "The measure of a man's real character is what he would do if he would never be found out" – and at the end of the day character is what counts when we tot up what we mean by 'success'.

~ 5 ~

Success May Begin –
Or End – At Home

> *Many a saint's reputation depends upon the silence of his family!*
>
> Anon.

*F*amilies can be funny – in more ways than one! When my daughter was born I had to tell my ten-year-old son that he couldn't see his mother and new sister straight away because of a hospital rule that only fathers could visit on the first day after a birth. The lad looked at me with that special scorn which sons and daughters sometimes reserve for their parents and then expostulated, "But you're only a relation by marriage; I'm a blood relation!"

Whether our relationships are by blood or marriage we would all want to make a success of them for much of our happiness depends upon doing so. Stephen Covey has written a book about the seven habits of effective families. In fact, we could ourselves probably think of many other habits that may help and try to develop them and encourage our families to do the same. But essentially, the emphasis on *giving* which in this volume I have applied to personal and business life is equally applicable to the domestic scene. Success in family life must depend upon a willingness to give – and sometimes give up or give way. How else can relational log-jams be cleared?

I have a whimsical little book called *How to Raise Your Parents* by Gordon McLean. Following are a few extracts written, I am sure, with tongue in cheek, but containing some grains of wisdom for all that.

> *Perhaps it is wise to remind you that good parents are developed, not born. Kids today have to have finely developed skills if they are going to succeed in raising good parents. Here are a few suggestions:*
>
> ***Encourage them.*** *Many parents are insecure in a world that is new to them and they often get confused and hesitant. You can encourage their hobbies.*
>
> ***Set a good example for adults by staying away from alcohol and tobacco.*** *Adults tend to copy the language, styles and tastes of the young.*
>
> ***Carefully watch their activities at home.*** *The effects of television on adults have not yet been fully established but certainly there is plenty of cause for concern.*
>
> ***Don't be too strict with your parents.*** *Parents should have leeway. They should have access to the phone, the stereo and the car – under carefully spelled out conditions, of course.*
>
> ***Remember, you are no bargain to live with either.*** *If there is one thing tougher than being a teenager, it's having one...*
>
> ***Say "Thank you" to each of your folks at least once a day.*** *They will survive the shock, and when they do they will be bragging everywhere about their wonderful teenager.*
>
> ***Learn how to say, "I am sorry".*** *Few things can lift the level of human relations like honest humility properly expressed.*

Happy Families

When I was a child we sometimes played a simple game called *Happy Families* with cards carrying, if I remember correctly, caricatures of such characters as Mr Bun the baker, Mrs Bun the baker's wife, Miss Bun the baker's daughter and Master Bun the baker's son.

Some might think that not only is the game outmoded but also the model on which it was based. Certainly, there has been a 'shuffling of the pack' and previously accepted 'norms' of family life have been called into question. Consider the context of family life in many first world countries.

Changes are apparent. For example, families are smaller. In Victorian times it was not unusual for parents to have ten or more children although infant mortality sometimes reduced the number who lived to maturity. Now, in China family size is restricted by government decrees while in western countries it may be limited for social or financial reasons.

Also, families are more mobile. It may be necessary for people to move – particularly to the cities – to find employment. This may mean that the extended family is less likely to be at hand. It is not only that grandparents no longer live with the family but also that uncles and aunts and cousins are often much further away. So, if young John is at odds with his dad he can't go next door for a wise word from Uncle George any more than teenage Mary can get to her understanding Auntie Flo. Instead there may need to be recourse to a social worker or counsellor.

It is also a fact that families have become more fragile. Marriage breakdowns are much more common than they used to be. If, sadly, holy wedlock degenerates into unholy deadlock there is less inclination to 'hang in', regardless. There is an emphasis on individualism and a tendency to be only committed to the provisional.

The effect on the children involved may be considerable although some remain remarkably resilient. It is argued that the separation of parents may be less traumatic for the youngsters than living with constant bickering. Be that as it may.

Many divorced people chose to remarry. That has been cynically called the "triumph of hope over experience". I would prefer to regard it as evidence of a deep longing for the stable relationships that can only come with commitment and the family values which should be the building blocks of society.

In a book entitled, *Family Policy: Government and Families in 14 Countries* I read "The family apparently is 'here to stay', recovering and adapting whatever the challenges from alternative life styles..." (The alternative life styles referred to included the communes set up in some countries.)

In a paper on social experiments in Australia I read that what is needed:

> *is not to break up the nuclear family but to open it up, surround it with support, give it greater flexibility and offer a wider variety of options for dealing with conflict and tension.*

Many people find that, for financial and social reasons, it is necessary for both parents to go out to work. The fact that so many cope as well as they do is remarkable but care is needed if family life is not to suffer. A home is meant to be something more than 'a parking place by night and an occasional filling station by day'.

What is Needed

As parents it is very easy to give our children what they ask for and not what they need and really crave. We may provide the computer games and mountain bikes and expensive toys – and that may be fine. But we also need to give of ourselves and address deeper needs.

In *Christus Victor* by my friends Denis and Pauline Hunter I came across the following *Beatitudes for Children* (source unknown):

> *Blessed is that child who has someone to believe in him (her) and has high hopes for him (her).*

Blessed is that child who has someone to whom he (she) can carry his (her) problems unafraid.

Blessed is that child whose home is a haven of happiness.

Blessed is that child to whom life is a book of knowledge and who is privileged to turn the pages one by one.

Blessed is that child who is allowed to pursue his (her) curiosity into every worthwhile field of information.

Blessed is that child who has someone who understands that childhood's griefs are real and bitter and call for understanding sympathy.

Blessed is that child who has learned freedom from selfishness through responsibility and cooperation.

The family is the assembly line of national character. Call that a 'motherhood' statement if you like, the fact remains that unless we can 'get things right' in the family we may well have concern for the future of the community at large. Many will feel, as I do, that spiritual values are even more important than the provision of material luxuries. A Roman Catholic maxim has been, "The family that prays together stays together". That doesn't always work out but it often does! (After more than four decades of marriage I can testify that a shared faith – along with shared work and interests – has been a tremendous strength for my wife and me and has helped to bind us together.)

There is need for mutualism and the principle of giving. It is natural that everyone in a family should hope to get something out of it – such as pleasure, security and support. But if in marriage and in family life we merely make demands and are preoccupied with our own wellbeing we are likely to be disappointed. On the other hand, if parents and children alike can give each other understanding, sympathy and love then success may come where, perhaps, it matters most – at home.

In my own childhood home there was a plaque with lines that still remain in my mind:

Love ever gives, forgives, outlives
And ever stands with open hands.
And while it lives it gives
For this is love's prerogative
To give and give and give.

~ 6 ~

Getting Airborne

> *We all live under the same sky but we don't all have the same horizon.*
>
> Konrad Adenauer

*I*t is my contention in this book that what gives lift-off to life and business is a determination to give, in one way or another. St Francis was expressing something of a paradox when he said, "It is in giving that we receive", but there are millions who have proved that he was right.

However, the problem for some people is that they have such low self-esteem and feel that they have so little to offer that they don't even give what they've got. Some firms also seem to have such little confidence in their products that their marketing is pathetic. So how can anyone rise above such feelings?

Two brief stories may help. The first is an American legend about an Indian brave who found an eagle's egg and put it in the nest of prairie chicken. The eaglet hatched with a number of chickens and grew up with them. Thinking he was a chicken he did as the others did, scratching around in the dirt and only fluttering and flying a metre or so above the ground. But one day he saw a magnificent bird high in the sky. "Whatever is that?" he asked.

"That is an eagle, the king of the birds" a prairie chicken clucked. "But don't give it a second thought, you could never be like him." And so the eagle remained grounded and lived and died without flying high because he thought that he was only a prairie chicken.

The other story is about a balloon seller who sought to attract a crowd of kids by releasing helium-filled balloons. He let go a white balloon and it floated upwards. He did the same with a red and then a yellow one. Kids rushed to buy the balloons. Then a small Negro boy asked, "If you filled a black balloon would it go up too?" "Sure" the man replied, "It's not the colour of the balloon but what's inside that counts."

Within us all there is much more potential than we may realise. We have something to offer which others need and in giving to them we will discover ourselves and realise the possibility of success. Some of the people who make the greatest contribution to the community are not loaded with talents; they just make better use of what they've got than others might do. Some of the firms that 'make it' do not necessarily have products any better than their competitors but they have the confidence to promote what they have so that it gains acceptance in the market-place.

Early Influences

The influences that play upon us as children can have a lasting effect. I remember that as a youngster I announced that I was going to be a doctor when I grew up. However, my mother immediately brought me down to earth with the comment, "That's not for the likes of you. We could never afford to pay what it would cost." Well, they were days of industrial depression and money was short. What is more, I am sure that my dear Mum never realised how her words got to me. But that enduring childhood memory indicates how easy it is to deflate a young person.

A more positive memory is that when I was young I used to feature in concerts as a boy soprano. Then when my voice broke my mother encouraged me to engage in elocution and dramatic presentations, as well as writing for local publications – something which gave me the confidence I needed and helped to prepare me for my work in later life. For that I am grateful.

It may be that we never quite climb out of the cradle or entirely leave behind the influences surrounding us in early life. But there are many illustrations of people who have risen above their beginnings and soared successfully, bringing satisfaction to themselves and benefit to other people.

A famous example would be Abraham Lincoln, who was born in a log cabin and whose father Thomas and stepmother Sarah were barely literate. Yet Abraham taught himself law and became one of the leading legal figures of his state. He entered politics and eventually became a great American president. A consuming passion of his was to help the downtrodden and one day as he stood in a slave market he cried, "If I ever get a chance to hit this thing I'll hit it hard!" The boy who was a nobody from nowhere became a somebody known everywhere. The Lincoln Memorial at the end of the Mall in Washington DC is a massive tribute in stone and I, with thousands of others, was moved to visit it. But an even more enduring memorial is Lincoln's place in the history and in the hearts of the American people.

The prestige of a presidency may not be ours. We may not become famous as high-fliers but we all have something worthwhile to offer. Success need not prove to be a mirage or an idle dream. If we work with what we've got we are likely to get – and give – more than we expect. Asked why she had succeeded while many of her peers had not, Dolly Parton said, "I never stopped trying and I never tried stopping".

Successive generations of English school children have had to memorise the words of *If* by Rudyard Kipling and that has been no bad thing. The poem includes the following lines:

> *If you can force your heart and nerve and sinew*
> *To serve your turn long after they are gone,*
> *And so hold on when there is nothing in you*
> *Except the Will which says to them: "Hold on!"*
> *...Yours is the earth and everything that's in it,*
> *And – which is more – you'll be a Man, my son!*

~ 7 ~

Welcome Complaints

> *The best time to deal with complaints is before they are made.*
>
> W.H.

*B*lessed is the business (or the individual) able to turn negatives into positives. Take complaints and criticism, for example. They may be blessings in disguise and provide chances to improve our service, whatever that may be.

Here I apply this thought to commercial activity in particular but it should not be difficult to translate it into the language of life at large and see how leaden complaints may point to golden opportunities to do things better. Even whingers may have their uses if they cause us to consider superior ways of giving something to our community!

I have discovered, to my cost, that some companies ignore complaints and feel that they are too busy to bother, but that is a dangerous attitude for in the final analysis the customer is sovereign. Complaints should be welcomed, even encouraged. Certainly, they should have careful examination for they are opportunities to learn how to improve the service and retain the goodwill of a customer.

If someone objects that this can take too much time and that time is money they might consider that customer retention may cost a lot less than customer acquisition. Some firms spend millions trying to get customers through the front door of their premises then hardly notice them disappearing through the back door!

The problem for a business is not the few customers who complain but the silent majority of dissatisfied people who quietly take their business elsewhere. A survey in the USA (by TARP of Washington, DC) showed that only 4 per cent of dissatisfied customers protested. But for every complaint received at company headquarters there were 26 people unhappy with their treatment. Between 65 per cent and 90 per cent of the 'silently unhappy' would never buy again from the company they felt had wronged them and, presumably, would talk to their friends about their experience, magnifying their negative reactions.

Another survey (for Travellers Insurance) indicated that only 9 per cent of non-complainers with a gripe involving $100 or more would buy from the company again whereas of those who did complain and had their problems addressed 82 per cent would purchase again. So it is wise to listen to complaints and be humble enough to learn from them if possible.

In business, giving satisfaction to customers may well be the secret of success. Charles Lazarus, Chief Executive of Toys 'R' Us said, "You just listen to the customers, then act on what they tell you". In boardrooms there are usually those who will speak up for shareholders and 'number crunchers' who will represent the big financial picture. But who speaks for the customers with whom the fate of the company will ultimately rest? Little customers may make companies big and their voices need to be heard in the corridors of power!

Contrasts

In 1982, Johnson and Johnson (manufacturers of medical supplies) suffered a serious blow when in the USA an unknown person put cyanide in some Tylenol capsules and killed five people. Within hours the company recalled the contaminated lot and the chairman of the company appeared in news conferences every half-hour to keep the public informed.

When a second incident occurred in another area all Tylenol was withdrawn around the country and two more contaminated pills were discovered. Johnson and Johnson could have said that the problem was a police matter outside its responsibility but, regardless of cost, it did not. Within a week it was redesigning Tylenol packaging with three tamper-resistant barriers and production of the new packaging began within a month.

A survey revealed that immediately after the poisoning half of Tylenol users said they would not use the product again but by 1985 the company had regained almost all of its 35 per cent share of the analgesic market. Wall Street analysts recognised that the company's sensitive response had helped retain the loyalty of millions of customers. It had turned a tragedy into a testimony to its concern for customers.

By way of contrast, there have been times when other firms have faced unexpected difficulties which may or may not have been of their making. Their main preoccupation has appeared to be self-justification with scant evidence of concern for customers who may have been hurt in one way or another. Fairly or unfairly, the public has felt that they were trying to weasel their way out of responsibility and have withdrawn their custom.

The clear truth is that, whatever the rights of wrongs of a case, no company can afford to even *appear* insensitive about the health and happiness of customers. It's possible to be right and yet wrong. That is, a company may not be at fault but it would be unwise for it to seem to be arrogantly dismissive of the perception of customers.

Checks on customer reaction should be searching and not merely casual. If in response to an enquiry a customer says, "Everything is fine but...", the 'but' should not be ignored. Even a slight hesitation in reply may indicate some concern. And what concerns a customer should concern the company. The danger is of only hearing what we expect to hear and not what we ought to hear.

In this chapter I am indebted to Richard C. Whiteley, author of *The Customer Driven Company*. He quotes psychologist Ellen Langer who claims that when businesspeople talk to customers they hear them say that the service was fine and they nod mindlessly instead of listening aggressively. Ms Langer suggests that they may have become mentally lazy – like children reacting to the following questions:

Q. *What do we call a tree that has acorns?*
A. *Oak.*

Q. *What do we call a funny story?*
A. *Joke.*

Q. *What do we call the sound made by a frog?*
A. *Croak.*

Q. *What do we call the white of an egg?*
A. *?*

Of course, the answer to the last question is, "The white", but many children (and adults?) get it wrong. They've got used to the 'oke' sound, and so they answer, "The yolk".

If businesspeople are customer-focused they will give full attention and listen with their 'third ear' being anxious to hear what people mean and not just what they say. Their main concern should be to ensure customer satisfaction.

I have said that complaints should be welcomed but I recognise that, human nature being what it is, we all like to bask in the warmth of compliments rather than feel cold, if bracing, blasts of criticism whether directed at us personally or at the organisation with which we are associated. Of course, the best time to deal with complaints is before they are made! The second-best time is as soon as possible after they have been made.

While criticism may sometimes be unfair and undeserved it does at least deserve due consideration. Honest explanation may take some of the sting out of a complaint and show the other side of a picture. If a genuine weakness is identified then the criticism may be as valuable as a nugget of gold and should be taken on board. The important thing is to try to deal with a problem, maintain a good relationship with a complainant – and then move on. That is, to turn a negative into a positive, which is important for those anxious to give their best.

~ 8 ~

Give Service

> *How can we ever be the sold short or the*
> *cheated, we who for every service have long*
> *ago been overpaid?*
>
> Meister Eckhart

I sometimes contact firms and get the impression that they are too big to bother. If I am not put off by recorded messages that do not address my need I have to listen to long sessions of piped music until eventually someone replies but makes me feel that my enquiry is an interruption of business rather than part of it. Sometimes my telephone calls are not returned and letters are not answered and I am driven to thumbing through the Yellow Pages telephone directory in search of another firm which might better meet my need.

Fortunately, I am not always caused to feel a grouch. My day is often made when members of staff are ready to go the extra mile in order to provide the service I require. I thank them profusely but their bosses should do the same for they are the kind of people who make and *keep* firms prosperous.

For example, the other day I took my car for a service and discovered that because of extra work to be done the job would take longer than expected. No public transport being available, I was glad when an official of the firm offered to take me to my home. At first I thought, "It's a big firm and they can afford to do things like that". Then I thought that perhaps it was because they did things like that they remained big. Without doubt, in the long run it pays to 'improve one's serve'.

In the handbook issued to passengers by a major airline the following statement appeared: "We have a motto, 'Our passengers are the purpose of our business – not an interruption in our work' and we shall try in every way to live up to it." The same booklet also stated, "The bell at the side of your seat will bring your steward or stewardess to you. You have only to ask. Their job is to make your flight comfortable and pleasant."

As a member of Rotary clubs in various parts of the world I made friends with some very successful business and professional men. I realised that their ideals regarding service had helped them to prosper materially but found that they were just as ready to give service when there was no monetary reward. In fact, I sometimes thought that they must have worked harder for nothing by way of material reward than they did for something of a financial nature. Service had become a way of life – not only a key to commercial success but a key to successful living.

General Norman Schwarzkopf was the US commander during the Desert Storm operation in Iraq. He has written as follows:

> *The Army with its emphasis on rank and medals and efficiency reports, is the easiest institution in the world to get consumed with ambition. Some officers spend all their time currying favour and worrying about their next promotion – a miserable way to live. But West Point saved me from that by instilling the ideal of service above self – to do my duty for my country even if it brought no gain at all. It gave me far more than a military career – it gave me a calling.'*

When I lived in the United Kingdom I met the Rev P.T.B ('Tubby') Clayton, the founder of the Toc H movement, widely known for its social service activities. Throughout his life Tubby Clayton rushed in where the straitlaced feared to tread, breaking conventions with happy abandon in order to be helpful. He said, "You have to help others. It is the way you pay the rent for your room on earth." But if he was right and service is the rent we pay for our room on earth I might ask myself whether at times I have been behind with the rent? I fear that I may have been!

We are all indebted to many who have served us well and whose names we may never know. For example, I remember a traumatic night when my wife was taken to hospital suffering from a severe loss of blood. Her life was saved by a transfusion made possible by a public-spirited donor for whom we fervently thanked God. An extension of this kind of service was indicated by a sticker I saw in a car. It read, "Don't take your organs with you – heaven knows they're needed here!" Through those who have responded to such appeals it has been possible for others to have organ transplants and an extension and improved quality of life. So service may be given even after one's own demise.

Beyond Price

There is some service that can be costed through a scale of professional fees or hourly rates but there are other expressions which are 'beyond price'. Dr Theodore Ferris told of a traveller in Africa who saw a nun dressing the ghastly wounds of a leper. He said, "I wouldn't do that for ten thousand dollars." She replied, "I wouldn't either."

In Brazil my wife and I visited some of the shanty towns with their huge populations of impoverished people. I went into some of the makeshift shacks which had to make do as homes. I saw the squalor and smelt the stench as children played in open sewers. In one place I was shown a thicket where, apparently, people who stepped out of line were shot on the orders of the controlling drug barons. Hearing the sound of firecrackers I wondered whether there was some celebration about to begin. I was told that it was simply a sign that a new supply of drugs had arrived.

But then in this hell on earth my wife and I met Margaret, a lovely young English woman, and some of her friends and was told that all they wanted was to live among the wretched inhabitants and serve them regardless of the threat to their own health and safety. What is more, they seemed radiantly happy at the prospect of doing so. Strangely, their gain was in loss. They seemed to be enriched as they embraced poverty. Their success was in the smile on a child's face or the gleam of hope in the eye of a careworn woman.

Not very many people would contemplate undertaking that kind of service but we may all be inspired by the example of those who do and in our modest way discover that service may be the key to any real success that we may have ourselves.

Sir Rabindranath Tagore, the Bengali Indian poet and mystic wrote:

I slept and I dreamt that life was all joy.
I awoke and I saw that life was but service.
I served and understood that service was joy.

~ 9 ~

Give Due Respect

> *If you wish others to respect you, you must show respect for them.*
>
> Ari Kiev

Among the definitions of the word 'respect' in *The Concise Oxford Dictionary* are the following: 'Regard with deference, esteem or honour; avoid degrading or insulting...treat with consideration, spare, refrain from... corrupting'.

In this chapter I will be emphasising the need to have due respect for people – whoever and whatever they may be. But first, let me include something about the need to have *respect for our natural environment*. There is no doubt that through a combination of thoughtlessness and selfishness human beings have done some terrible things to planet Earth and we owe a debt to those who have called attention to environmental issues. Sometimes they have been as a 'voice crying in the wilderness' and their message has been disregarded, and for that there may be a price to pay.

Sometimes political leaders have had to balance short-term considerations such as employment and economic well-being with long-term concerns about, for example, pollution. No doubt, political life wasn't meant to be easy! But when all is said and done, having due respect for our environment must be a priority for our own sake and for the sake of those who will follow us.

Concern for the environment should include *a proper respect for our own bodies*. Through the years I have had contact with many affected by substance abuse and have been saddened to see the ways in which their bodies have been wrecked by their addictions. Some, especially among younger folk, have been loud in their protests on environmental issues but seemingly have been unable to resist ravaging their own health and perhaps that of other people through their indulgence. Trying to help them has been worthwhile though often discouraging work.

It is amazing how silly intelligent people can be. While knowing full well that certain actions could endanger their lives they persist in disregarding all advice as though they were uniquely indestructible. For instance, in Australia there is a widespread problem with skin cancer and publicity campaigns have urged people to 'cover up' and avoid over-exposure to the strong rays of the sun. Yet, by way of example, I have a young friend who still works out of doors a lot of his time, often with much of his body exposed, even though possible signs of melanoma are apparent and members of his family are very concerned. We may not want to cosset ourselves unduly but sense and self-respect would surely call for reasonable care.

I contend that *giving due respect to other people* is an essential ingredient of a successful life. Everyone deserves respect as a human being – created in the image of God as the Judaeo/Christian tradition would affirm. Anything that devalues people as people must ultimately be counter-productive.

They Can Do

Then *people should receive due respect for what they know and what they can do*. In a thought-provoking comment Ralph Waldo Emerson wrote, "Every man I meet is in some way superior and I can learn of him" (which of course equally applies to women).

Most of the people I know can do some things far better than I could do them. For example, I think of the little old granny with an ability to crochet – something about which I wouldn't have a clue! Then I think of fellows who could hardly put a pen to paper but who, in their knowledge of the land and its cultivation, would leave me for dead. I think of people who seem to have an almost instinctive understanding of mechanical matters – things about which my ignorance would be so great as to be distinguished! All these skills evoke my respect and admiration and remind me that although we may all be very different we all have a contribution to make to the community.

Everybody has a niche that they were meant to fill –
A corner of the universe in which to do God's will;
Everybody has a task, a mission on the earth,
A chance to use or waste the gifts bestowed on them at birth.

People should be respected for their potential. I have read of a German scholar who would always salute his class of young students before delivering a lecture. When asked the reason he replied, "I am saluting the future great men (or women) of my nation". Thomas Carlyle said, "A great man shares his greatness by the way he treats little men". In fact, some who may appear to have little knowledge or experience may have tremendous capacity which is deserving of respect.

There will be times when all of us are not at our best for a variety of reasons. Our true potential will not always be immediately apparent but to quote Ralph Waldo Emerson again, "Every man [or woman] is entitled to be valued by his [or her] best moments".

Then *people should be respected for their experience.* 'Ageism' is all too common in western society. If age is often venerated in the east it is just as often denigrated in the west and a kind of apartheid based on age can operate. Younger people can look at the elderly in such a way that they feel as though they must be invisible!

Now, I love the freshness and the enthusiasm of youth and count many young people among my friends and learn from them. But all wisdom was not born with their generation! Those who have 'been there and done that' may have learnt something along the way and deserve respect for having borne the heat and burden of the day.

Of course, if we expect others to respect us we must demonstrate our respect for them. If older people are forever putting down the younger generation they should not be surprised if their lack of respect is reflected back to them. Bridging the cultural chasm between generations is not always easy but sincere attempts at mutual understanding may well bear abundant fruit.

The last (but not the least) ones deserving of our respect may be ourselves as persons. All too often we may put ourselves down and sell ourselves short – and then be surprised if people take us at our own valuation. I talked to a gifted woman who, whenever she forgot anything or made some small slip told herself that she was stupid – and believed it. When I remarked on this and tried to suggest that she should take a more positive view of herself, she said that as a child she was always being told that she was silly and the thought had become ingrained in her thinking. What a pity!

In some ways self-respect is our birth right; in other ways it may have to be earned. But certainly, it is within the realm of possibility for all of us. We may not be able to rewrite the start to our life story but at least we can resolve to seek the grace to make sure that it has a good ending.

Edgar Guest wrote:

> *I have to live with myself, and so*
> *I want to be fit for myself to know,*
> *I want to be able, as days go by,*
> *Always to look myself straight in the eye...*
>
> *Whatever happens, I want to be*
> *Self-respecting and conscience free.*

~ 10 ~

Give An Ear

> *We have been given two ears and one mouth but are sometimes slow to take the hint.*
>
> W.H.

Much has been written about how we can talk our way to success. Perhaps more should be written about *listening* our way to success! Former US President Lyndon B. Johnson had a notice in his office which read, "You 'aint learnin' nothin' when you're doin' all the talkin'." Despite the dubious grammar, there may be more than a grain of wisdom in that saying and a few present-day politicians might take it to heart.

One of the most common complaints about some of our political leaders is that they "do not listen to the people". Now the extent to which the complaint is justified may be debatable but the importance of listening is not.

In a senior management/leadership role I was called upon to do a lot of public speaking but I learnt that it was at least equally vital that I *listened* to other people, heard about their ideas for the organisation and their reports of what was happening in centres across a large country, often balancing one version of events with another. Listening may take time but failure to listen may cost money and much more.

Sam Walton was the founder of Wal-Mart and one of the richest men in America. He once flew in a plane to Mt. Pleasant, Texas, landed and gave instructions to his co-pilot to meet him about a hundred miles down the road. Then he drove in a Wal-Mart truck the rest of the way so that he could chat with the driver and pick up his perceptions about the business. Sam Walton was a top executive who believed in being in touch with the proverbial grass roots of his massive organisation.

By way of contrast, I have known fast-talking salespeople so caught up with their standard sales pitch that they have not bothered to listen to what customers might have to say about their needs. They should have known that while it is easy to talk yourself out of a sale you will be far less likely to *listen* yourself out of one!

Making Friends

We may have made the mistake of thinking that we will make friends with people when we impress them with what we have to say. In fact, we are more likely to make friends by encouraging people to express how *they* feel. The greatest good we can do for someone may not be through sharing the riches of our knowledge but in helping them discover and then share their own riches. People are more likely to remember what they have told us than what we have told them.

We show respect for someone when we really listen to them The ability to listen may be the key to a beautiful friendship. Our respect is likely to evoke the respect of the other person and mutual respect can easily blossom into friendship. There are so many people ready to talk at us, including the gurus on the radio or TV. But when we are 'up against it' the cry of our hearts may be for someone ready to listen to us – really listen, that is. And I have discovered that need in rich as well as poor people, educated as well as uneducated folk.

I came across these verses by an anonymous author:

> When I ask you to listen to me
> And you start giving advice,
> You have not done what I asked.

When I ask you to listen to me
And you begin to tell me
Why I shouldn't feel that way,
You are trampling on my feelings.

When I ask you to listen to me
And you feel you have to do *something*
To solve my problems
You have failed – strange as it may seem.

Listen!
All I asked was that you listen.
Not talk or do. Just hear me...

Creative listening is an art. It not only encourages someone to articulate their problems but feel the way to their own custom-made solutions. That kind of listening may take some doing. Paradoxically, it may take more than just our ears. It may involve our hearts and minds, our hands and eyes – indeed, our total body language. It may mean listening with what has been called our 'third ear' and hearing what isn't said as well as what is. And that can be hard work.

Former President Ronald Reagan told a humorous and probably apocryphal story about a senior and a junior psychiatrist. They each turned up at work in a morning and received their patients. By the evening the younger man was nearly worn out while the older one was completely fresh. The younger man asked his colleague how he could see so many patients and yet remain fresh. The older doctor replied, "It's easy. I never listen."

Seriously, I once had a boss like that. He would breeze up and say, "How are you?" – but he never waited for an answer. I was young at the time and being capable of facetiousness was tempted to call after the great man, "I'm about to drop dead" – but he probably wouldn't have heard anyway!

Whether in business or professional life or in personal relationships, success may well depend on our willingness to give a listening ear. Although we were given two ears and one mouth we are sometimes very slow to take the hint. I guess we'll just have to work on it.

~ 11 ~

Give Space

> *He brought me forth also into a large place.*
>
> The Bible; King James Version

*I*t may be a sign that I am growing older but some of the current pop songs seem easily – and perhaps desirably – forgettable. On the other hand, some snatches of tunes and lines of lyrics from yesteryear can float back into consciousness and be welcomed. For example, I remember a song with the line, "Give me land, lots of land – don't fence me in". Perhaps we all share that sentiment at times – when we feel cramped by life's little spaces and hemmed in by circumstances.

In our private lives we need personal space. A truly loving relationship should not be stifling or claustrophobic. It should allow room for the development of individuality and, paradoxically, the best and the closest relationships do allow for this. If we want to make a success of our marriage and family life we may need to learn this lesson and give space.

Parents with youthful sons and daughters often have to maintain a critical balance. On the one hand they want to be protective but at the same time they have to give their young folk space – difficult as that may seem, at times. Having helped our children to grow, we have to be prepared to let them go. When they drop out of the nest and seem to be in free-fall our hearts may be in our mouths but we have to give them space, while still letting them know that we are 'there for them'.

In Business

Now the same principle may apply in business or professional life. We may need to give space to others. I have an acquaintance who has built up a one-man business as an interior designer. He has worked hard and prospered but now, in a sense, he is the victim of his own success. He has more work than he can handle and customers are becoming exasperated by his repeated failure to deliver on time, if at all. He is like a juggler with too many balls in the air.

Clearly he is faced with two alternatives. He can settle for the status quo and maintain his hands-on operation or he can take on staff and give space to others in a larger enterprise. For him it seems to be a difficult decision and I can understand the reasons for that. Giving space to others may sometimes seem perilous and painful yet often it becomes essential. It is a matter of moving from doing the job to managing the job.

In *Developing the Leaders Around You* John C. Maxwell has written:

> *Not having the time to teach another person to do a job is probably the most common reason people give for not delegating. And not delegating is probably the most common reason people do not have time. Inability to delegate due to lack of time is short-term thinking. Time lost on delegating on the front end is recovered at the back end.*

Anyone building an organisation must learn to multiply themselves by means of delegation, networking or whatever. They cannot be in two places at once. They cannot encompass all that needs to be done. They must invest time and effort in training carefully selected people who will ensure that the organisation's mission is advanced.

An old Chinese proverb went like this:

> *If you want one year of prosperity,*
> *grow grain.*
> *If you want ten years of prosperity*
> *grow trees*
> *If you want one hundred years of prosperity,*
> *grow people.*

Delegation is not the same as abdication and supervision will still be necessary with an expectation of accountability. Yet space must be given to people if the organisation is to breathe and folk are to use their initiative. Another word for what I have in mind is 'empowerment' and the paradox is that in empowering others we do not necessarily lose power ourselves. Yet in another sense, of course, if we share responsibility we must also share authority and the ability to achieve. The safeguard is in careful selection of effective people and assiduously mentoring them.

Peter Drucker wrote, "No executive has ever suffered because his subordinates were strong and effective". But to be effective people must be given adequate space within the accepted framework of the organisation. They will not *always* perform as well as their leader but if they do the job 80% as well then the delegation will probably be worthwhile. In any case, if subordinates fail because their leader has tied their hands behind their backs the failure is not really theirs but his (or hers).

W. Alton Jones affirmed:

> *The man (or woman) who gets the most satisfactory results is not always the man (or woman) with the most brilliant single mind, but rather the man (or woman) who can best coordinate the brains and talents of his (or her) associates.*

And that must involve giving them space to grow.

As a child my wife lived in China where her parents worked for many years. Among her souvenirs she still has a pair of tiny shoes no more than between nine and ten centimetres in length. They were once worn by an adult woman whose feet had been bound when she was young to prevent them from growing, such tiny feet being considered fashionable before the inhumane practice was outlawed.

In some situations in our society people may be cruelly cramped by conventions or bound by bureaucratic restrictions. Our success may be in giving them space to grow and walk the road to fulfilment and usefulness.

~ 12 ~

Give Time

> *The important thing is not the number of years given to a man but what he does with them.*
>
> William Slim

Our most valuable asset is not the money we have in the bank, the house in which we live or the car that sits in the garage. It is something of which we have a limited amount and something which cannot be hoarded but must be used on an hourly basis. It is time.

So what do we do with this commodity? A time management study released by *USA Today* indicated, surprisingly perhaps, that during his or her career the average American worker would be likely to spend six months sitting at red lights, one year searching for belongings amid the clutter of home or office, eight months opening junk mail, five years waiting in lines and six years eating. Quite a thought!

Peter Drucker wrote: "Nothing else, perhaps, distinguishes effective executives as much as their tender loving care of time". We live in an era when there is a proliferation of time-saving gadgets and I find no fault with that. But how do we use all the time that is saved? We may be replete with labour-saving devices but are we any wiser in the way we use the time they release for us? Then how generous are we in giving of our most valuable asset to others who may need our help?

In *The Business Handbook* by Dexter R. Yager Sr I read the following lines by an unknown author:

> *Take time to live;*
> > *it is one secret of success.*
> *Take time to think;*
> > *it is the source of power.*
> *Take time to play;*
> > *it is the secret of youth.*
> *Take time to read;*
> > *it is the foundation of knowledge.*
> *Take time for friendship;*
> > *it is the source of happiness.*
> *Take time to laugh;*
> > *it helps lift life's load.*
> *Take time to dream;*
> > *it hitches the soul to the stars.*
> *Take time to worship;*
> > *it is the highway to reverence.*
> *Take time to pray;*
> > *it helps bring God near*
> > *and washes the dust of earth from our eyes.*

I have written elsewhere about time management in general (see for example in *Nice Guys Can Win*) but here I would share further thoughts related to the general theme of this book. Time can very easily get away from us so that at the end of a week we wonder where it has all gone. Time can be filched even by well-meaning friends, unless we are careful. But success in most fields comes with a price tag on it and often the main cost is in terms of time.

For example, someone anxious to build a business may have to spend less time in front of the 'telly' exercising little apart from the thumb on the clicker! It may be necessary to forgo the 'horizontal inspiration' of the long lie-in. There is 'no gain without pain' and it may be necessary to give extra time to a business in order to have more time later in life for the family or for favourite pursuits. That is fair enough but it will take dedication and discipline on a daily basis. On the other hand, for some who make their work their life it may be necessary to cut back work hours or leave work on time rather than stay late, in order to have more time to spend with their family. Failure to manage time is probably the biggest stumbling block on the path to success.

Not Only Making Money

For some people success is not only in making money but in then being able to use it to support worthy causes. I talked to one wealthy man like that who told me how he enjoyed using his money for charitable causes – sometimes, I suspect, doing good by stealth through anonymous donations. There are those for whom success has not been so much in dollars and cents but in educational achievements, for instance. They have paid the price in time and effort and academic honours have been theirs and they have then, hopefully, been able to use their knowledge to help others.

Some, having proved a point and achieved success in one field feel that they should give it away for one reason or another. In these days people are discovering 'late vocations'. The top Australian jockey Darren Beadman is an up-to-date example of this. At thirty-two years of age and at the height of his career he decided to seek success of a different kind as a minister of religion. As one newspaper put it, he turned one of Shakespeare's most famous lines on its head by giving up his horse for a kingdom – the kingdom of God!

In another generation there was Jenny Lind, the 'Swedish nightingale' who, at the height of her fame, decided to step down from the operatic stage. She would not have claimed to have been a saint by any means but when asked why she had renounced the glamour of the footlights she picked up her Bible and said, "Because I found it left me so little time for this and" – pointing to the sunset – "none for that".

One of my heroes as a youth was Albert Schweitzer, a brilliant European academic with a worldwide reputation in the fields of philosophy, theology and music. He felt that he should leave behind his assured career, study to become a doctor of medicine and go to one of the poorest parts of Africa to build a hospital with his own hands and then give years of service to very needy people.

How we give our time is a very individual thing and what is right for one may not be right for another. The important thing is to give our time in balanced and purposeful ways and not allow it to get away from us like water spilt on sand. None of us can be sure how much time we will be given. Everybody tends to think that every one is mortal apart from themselves. In fact, we are all mortal and we had better believe it – although the important thing is not the number of years we have but what we do with them.

Will Rogers was known as the 'cowboy philosopher'. He was asked, "If you only had 48 hours to live, how would you spend them?" He replied, "One at a time". That is all any of us can do. But if we are wise in the way we spend time by the hour there will be little doubt that the aggregation of hours which is our life will deserve a tick for success.

~ 13 ~

Give An Example, Plus

> As I grow older, I pay less attention to what men say. I just watch what they do.
>
> Andrew Carnegie

During the Second World War, after the evacuation from Dunkirk, some French troops were lying down, thoroughly dispirited, at an English port. Unlike their British allies they had not only lost a campaign but a country. Then another ship came in and from it stepped a company of the brigade of Guards. Their tradition of 'spit and polish and stiff upper lip' seemed indestructible; they actually held a kit inspection on the beach at Dunkirk! As they stepped off the ship they were as smart as it was possible to be under the circumstances and they marched off with the same precision as if they were changing the guard at Buckingham Palace.

A listless-looking Frenchman saw what was happening then suddenly got to his feet, swung up his pack, squared his shoulders, fell in and marched away behind the Guards. His compatriots suddenly looked up and did the same, for a powerful example had changed an understandably dispirited company of men into self-respecting soldiers again.

People are usually more ready to follow footsteps than advice. What people are and what they do will speak more loudly than anything they say. Certainly, modelling of character or ability is more likely to evoke a positive response than any amount of criticism.

I have studied many management manuals and listened to plenty of lectures on leadership but I think that I have learnt more from observing competent managers and first-rate leaders in action. Example has been more motivational than precept. It has been particularly instructive to observe how leaders have performed under pressure. There has been as much to learn from reactions as from actions. Of course, a poor example can also have a powerful influence. I have read that Dick Shepherd, once the greatly-loved vicar of St Martins-in-the-Fields Church in London's Trafalgar Square, nearly gave away the idea of entering the ministry because he saw a parson lose his temper at a game of tennis!

Now the fact that we have all been influenced in one way or another by the example of other people should indicate that, unconsciously perhaps, our example will also affect other folk and particularly the young. The realisation that our success could set up a positive chain reaction in other people may be an added incentive for us to make that extra effort. As John Donne put it, "No man is an island". So giving a good example may be an important part of being a success.

I came across the following lines by an unnamed author:

One good man teaches many, men believe what they behold.
One deed of kindness noticed is worth forty that are told.
He who stands with men of honour, learns to hold his honour
dear,
For right living speaks a language which to everyone is clear,
Though an able speaker charms me with eloquence – I say...
I'd rather see a sermon, than hear one any day.

Not Enough?

But example alone may not be enough. In fact, example can even be daunting. Many great pianists have also been teachers and have had their own particular methods. The composer Chopin would be a case in point. One of his pupils said of him, "His only method was to play like an angel and then tell me to do likewise". Of course, such an instruction was hopeless unless one happened to have the genius of a Chopin.

So, to the powerful influence of example something may need to be added. I mean *coaching*. Many of us not only need people who will say, "Do as I say" or even, "Do as I do". We need people who will get alongside us and be patient when at times we fail and falter. Coaches are people who are 'there for us' helping us to realise that the only real failure is a failure to try again – and again. And if, at times we need 'mentoring', we can be sure that there will always be times when someone will need us to coach them. The extent to which we help others to succeed may well be the measure of our own success.

Doctors Les and Leslie Parrott are marriage counsellors who sometimes recommend people to link up with a marriage mentor couple – perhaps older people who have worked through problems in their own lives. They received the following letter from a newly-married couple who had consulted them:

Dear Les and Leslie,

How can we ever thank you for helping us find a marriage mentor couple! Our 'mentoring' relationship with Nate and Sharon ended up being the most important thing we have ever done to build up our marriage. It was nice to have another couple know what we were going through and remain objective at the same time.

Some day we hope to give back the gift that Nate and Sharon gave to us by 'mentoring' some newly-married couples. We think that every couple just starting should have a mentor.

People who can be 'examples plus' are important in many circumstances. My wife and I visited Tijuana, Mexico and there met a blind young man called Miguel. He had just won a marathon race and was clutching a trophy in recognition of the victory. His face was alight with pride and ecstasy and we were thrilled with him, particularly as we thought about the limitations imposed by his lack of sight. I enquired about this and then discovered the story behind the story. His keen young minister who was with him and was so loud in his praise had been Miguel's mentor and trainer. In fact he had run with him, guiding and encouraging him and only holding back as they reached the finishing line so that Miguel might be the one to breast the tape. So whose was the success? In reality the victory was a shared one.

Commitment

Coaching or 'being there' for someone else will call for caring and commitment but it may be the way to success in developing relationships, building a business or helping to strengthen a community. 'Mentoring' may be the way to personal or corporate growth. If people or institutions are not growing they are likely to be dead – mentally or spiritually. If they think that they are full grown they need someone to help them think again.

It is all too easy to settle for the status quo and accept mediocrity as a norm. St Francis Xavier said, "Give up your small ambitions" which I take to be another way of saying that people should 'think big'. But often a person needs someone else to help them lift their sights. They need a mentor to encourage them to do what they may not want to do in order that they might be what, deep down, they really want to be.

Selfridges is one of the largest department stores in London. It was built up by H. Gordon Selfridge who had the following words to say about leadership and coaching:

> *The boss drives his men, the leader coaches them. The boss depends upon authority, the leader on goodwill. The boss inspires fear, the leader inspires enthusiasm. The boss says 'I', the leader says 'we'. The boss fixes the blame for the breakdown, the leader fixes the breakdown. The boss says 'Go', the leader says 'Let's go'.*

A man I knew who became the head of a large international movement said that, when he was a young man, the then head of the organisation said to him, "I'm going to scrape your bones!" He had the temerity to ask the great man whether an ambulance would be needed! He was told to 'wait and see'. In fact, the subsequent interview lived up it its operational forecast. The wise older man got his younger colleague 'on the raw' and took him to task on a few points but the negatives were in a positive context and part of an ongoing preparation for the great responsibilities which were to come. With criticism there was warm encouragement to 'walk tall' and 'walk straight'.

Success may lie not only in what we achieve personally but in what we enable others to achieve even after we have finished our stint. In a relay race it is not enough for a competitor to run a fast lap; he or she must pass on the baton to someone else or in the end the race will be lost. So too, through a good example and wise 'mentoring' we may not only multiply our contribution in the present but extend our helpful influence into the future. And that sounds like success!

~ 14 ~

Give Value

> *The most profitable deal is the one in which no-one loses.*
>
> W.H.

I was intrigued to come across an old advertisement, apparently from an English periodical published in Victorian times. It read:

DRESSES
Neat, modest

Serges, cashmeres and merinos
will not fade
Prices
18/-, 21/- & 24/6

Others
THAT WILL FADE
at lower prices

It might be argued that garments that would fade should not have been sold anyway but at least there was an attempt to uphold self-imposed advertising standards and not mislead customers. Anything worthy of being called success must always involve trying to give value to other people. In this chapter I focus on commercial activity but the principle can be translated into the language of life as a whole.

A cartoon showed a company president announcing to his staff, "Gentlemen, this year the trick is honesty." From across the table a vice-president gasped, "Brilliant!" while another vice-president muttered, "But so risky." Risky or not, I detect in management literature an increased emphasis on maintaining business ethics. There is a realisation that, apart from anything else, short-changing is likely to prove counter-productive for the firms concerned and undermine confidence in the community at large.

There were 1,300 top executives who responded to a survey to identify the human qualities necessary for business success. Seventy-one per cent put integrity as the top of 16 traits which would enhance an executive's effectiveness. Now *I* would say that honesty is the best policy simply because it is right but obviously it can be contended that it is also good for business. Certainly, the best advertisement a firm can have is a satisfied customer and the worst one is a person who feels that he or she has been sold-short. The multiplied resentment of people not receiving value for money can be like an acid eating away the reputation of a company but appreciation for a good product can contribute to an atmosphere in which sales can climb.

Many manufacturers now realise that 'value' is not only something to be assessed according to definitions they have developed on their own but as customers define it. By way of example, I was recently one of a group asked to spend a day giving opinions on the features we considered most important in cars. We were not a collection of automobile experts but as car owners what we thought important was to be taken into consideration. After all, we – and the other car buyers we represented – would be the final arbiters on what the manufacturers might produce. It was important for car makers to know what we thought was valuable as well as to listen to the technocrats.

Value to a customer will depend on *product* quality and *service* quality. What is produced must be of high quality, but that is not all. A product might be excellent but if it is not delivered on time it could, under certain circumstances be almost worthless. If a machine arrives too late to do the job for which it was ordered then its value may well be diminished. The same sort of thing could be said about promised after-sales service. If the promised 'back-up' is not provided then value could be greatly reduced.

Let me give a small personal illustration. For the second year running I went to a firm at the beginning of November to order a refill diary for my 'planner'. And for the second year, well into January, it still hadn't arrived, despite all assurances. When I complained I was told that my experience was 'about average' – which didn't say much for supply standards! After all, where value is concerned timing can be of the essence.

As a general rule, it is better to under-promise and over-deliver rather than the other way around. Having said that, I realise of course that sometimes a person may make promises in good faith and then not be able to keep them because of factors outside their control. However, giving value must include being ready, if necessary, to 'burst a boiler', as the saying goes, in order to honour assurances.

Many Factors Make Up Value

Obviously many factors have to be taken into account when considering the value of goods and services. In addition to the cost of raw materials and production there is the cost of distribution. It is said that on some items more than 60 per cent of what is paid at the supermarket check-out may go on getting the item from the point of manufacture to the customer's basket. That involves jobs, the profits of 'middlemen', transport and so on. Many customers perceive value in being able to see and handle their possible purchases, and to enjoy the ambience and the amenities of a store while they make their choice. This all makes up an invisible price tag, but so be it.

In the future, consumer patterns may well change, with home shopping taking an ever-larger share of the market, selection being from TV screens or catalogues rather than supermarket shelves. As with home banking, some people may find this to be time-saving and more convenient. In the meantime, someone is paying for the megastores and the acres of car-parking space provided for the convenience of customers. A saying in the north of England is, 'There's nowt for nowt', and in many ways it is true.

In the commercial field giving customers value for money and even a little more than they expect may be a recipe for long-term success. Stanley Marcus, himself a retailer, put it rather well when he wrote, obviously with commerce in mind:

> *There are only two things of importance. One is the customer, and the other is the product. If you take care of customers, they come back. If you take care of your product, it doesn't come back. It's just that simple. And it's just that difficult.*

However, giving value is not only a recipe for commercial success. This thing is bigger than business; it's as large as life. We should all be into it, making a contribution to our community in all kinds of ways. The extent to which we do that may be hard to measure but significant nonetheless. Our true success will lie in not only helping ourselves but others as well, for success is in giving.

~ 15 ~

Give It Your Best Shot

> *Even if there is a crock of gold at the foot of the rainbow we will probably have to dig for it.*
>
> W.H.

When encouraging me to be industrious my father often claimed, "No-one ever died of hard work." Whether that statement was literally true I am not sure. What I do believe is that people who have made a success out of life have not only needed all the grace they could get but, in most cases, have also had to work hard or give it their best shot, as the saying goes.

Success and its achievement may not be an exact science but generally it doesn't come without effort. I have written elsewhere in this book about the importance of having a dream but here I would emphasise that making a worthy dream come true is likely to call for what Winston Churchill described as blood, sweat and tears.

Bill Wyllie is a prominent businessman in Perth, WA. He has been active in Singapore and Hong Kong as well as in Australia and has enjoyed outstanding success in rescuing ailing companies and, in some cases, turning multi-million dollar losses into multi-million dollar profits. *Time* magazine described him as "South-East Asia's most effective corporate doctor" and in 1993 he was appointed a Member of the Order of Australia for his services to business and commerce.

In addition to success in business he has worked tirelessly for various charities helping, for example, to raise millions of dollars for The Salvation Army. Had he not been so successful in getting he could not have been so effective in giving. But he was not born with the proverbial silver spoon in his mouth. As an eight-year-old he himself spent some time in a Salvation Army boys' home. When he was 12 he was delivering telegrams after school and his 15 shillings wage paid the weekly rent for the family home. Then he got a second job delivering newspapers and doubled his income. He left school at 13 but studied at nights in order to gain qualifications. Life has not always been easy for Bill. His first wife died and a son was killed in a climbing accident. Yet the list of his achievements is impressive and his success is obvious.

A Chinese journalist in Hong Kong said, "Mr Wyllie, you have been extraordinarily lucky. Chinese people feel that they should follow you on the stock market." Bill replied, "Yes I have been lucky. But I have noticed that the harder I work the luckier I get." For Bill the secret has been more in pluck than in luck.

Loved Work

Oft-quoted is the Jerome K. Jerome character who said that he loved work so much that he could sit and watch it for hours! Now hopefully, life is not so grim and we are not so stuffy that we can't appreciate the humour in what he said. Bad for us if we are! But for all that the character in question may be an unlikely model for would-be achievers!

J. M. Barrie wrote:

> *I knew three undergraduates who lodged together in a dreary house at the top of a dreary street. Two of them used to study until two in the morning while the third slept.*
>
> *When they shut their books they awoke number three who rose and dressed and studied until breakfast*

time; among the many advantages of this system was that, as they were dreadfully poor, one bed did for the three of them.

Two of them occupied it at one time and the third at another. Terrible privation? Dreadful destitution? Not a bit of it. If knowledge was at the top of 100 steps, if students occasionally died of hunger and hard work combined, if midnight oil burned to show a ghastly face, weary and worn, if lodgings were cheap and dirty and dinners were few and far between, life was real and earnest, and it did not turn out to be an empty dream.

At the other end of the life-span was Pablo Casals, the world famous 'cellist. When he was 83 it was reported that he was asked why he continued to practise four or five hours a day. He replied, "Because I think I am making progress." Even as an old man he was still prepared to work hard in order to reach higher heights of achievement and deeper depths of understanding – and then give inspiration to others through his music.

Some people hope to stumble on success without having to make any effort but in real life it rarely happens that way. Success doesn't usually drop out of the sky. There is a price to pay and effort to be made. Even if there is a crock of gold at the foot of the rainbow we will probably have to dig for it! Although faith can move mountains a spade may also be needed. And we'd better believe it.

A Sense of Direction

Success in most fields may demand the sacrifice of sterile leisure and a willingness to work harder and longer than other people. But there is more to it than that. Some who work hard never seem to achieve very much for themselves or other people. They simply go from bed to work and from work to bed in never-ending drudgery. Life for them is like a treadmill and they never seem to get far.

There may be many reasons for that but one could be *the lack of a sense of direction and goals*.

Personally, I have found it important to have both *long-term and short-term goals*, written down and referred to often. Then fairly regularly, when I have been charging around doing this and that, I have had to pull myself up and check the extent to which my efforts have been focused and related to my stated goals.

Sometimes we may need to stop and, so to speak, take our glasses off and look at them as well as through them. They may need changing. Perhaps we should have another way of looking at things. The way we look at a problem may be the problem. To change the figure of speech, we may be climbing a ladder, rung by rung, without checking whether it is leaning against the right wall!

Our long-term goals may or may not be related to material gain. For example, one person may be motivated by a desire to be effective in their calling as a priest, another by a desire to achieve academic or artistic excellence. Others may indeed be 'grabbed' by the thought of having enough money to retire early, spend more time with family, travel or make significant contributions to worthy causes.

In business it is important to have a bifocal vision of people and money. Some can't see the accounts for the people and others can't see the people for the accounts.

Only big ambitions will inspire big efforts over the long haul. People are more likely to fall by the wayside because of under-motivation than because of over-strain, but by hard work for worthwhile ends we may increase our capacity to help ourselves and contribute to the lives of others which, I contend in this book, is the hallmark of the best kind of success. (George Bernard Shaw described a gentleman as "a man who puts into the common stock a little more than he takes out." That may be a tall order, bearing in mind our indebtedness to so many people, but it is a worthy aim for all that.)

There is also the need for short-term goals – horizons to beckon us on, incentives for service, staging posts on the road of success. For some, the short-term aim may be an idyllic holiday in Hawaii with the family – and that sounds good. For others it might mean being able to afford a new car. For someone else it might be earning a university degree or some other honour or recognition – anything that is within our power to achieve and not dependent entirely on someone else.

There may also be value in having even shorter short-term goals – that is, specific goals for a week or a day. Writing them in a 'planner' may help to keep us on track although we may need to build into our planning a degree of flexibility in order to cope with unexpected demands.

Then with the need for focus and clear goals there may be *the need to work smart*. Someone learning to swim may expend enormous effort and make slow progress while another who has been well coached may go further and faster with less effort. In order to work smart we need to give attention to *how* we do things and whether there may not be better ways. As the old adage had it, we should use our heads to save our legs.

Some have the ability to work hard and yet be relaxed at the same time; it is an enviable gift. St Augustine described God as he conceived him to be in four Latin words which may be translated into the six English words, "Always at work, always at rest". In that pithy statement there may be an ideal to which in some degree we might ourselves aspire.

~ 16 ~

Give a Thought!

> *The chief purpose of the body is to carry the brain around.*
>
> Thomas Edison

Thomas Edison was an inventor with more than a thousand patents to his credit and the founder of what later became the General Electric Company. Obviously he was a man with plenty of 'runs on the board' and, after years of contemplating human nature, his caustic comment was, "Five per cent of the people think. Ten per cent of the people think they think. The other eighty-five per cent would rather die than think."

Bertrand Russell, philosopher and Nobel prizewinner, came to the same conclusion. He said, "There is nothing men fear so much as thought." Yet an ability to give thought would seem to be essential for success.

If we asked a carpenter what he was making and he said that he had no idea we might question his sanity. Yet many live without ever questioning what life is all about – which does seem rather dumb. We may not possess super intellects but at least we can use the brains we've got, which may well be enough to put us ahead!

For a start, we might give some thought to the universe of which we are a part. Is it the product of chance or does it give evidence of design and order? If it does, why? We might give thought to ourselves as human beings. What are we? Who are we? Whose are we?

Then what about the mystery of life? We may wonder: is life like a black chessboard with white squares on it or a white board with black squares on it? In other words, is it basically bad or good? To change the figure of speech, is life a grimy bubble liable to burst or an egg full of untold possibilities? Science looks for a pattern; religion looks for purpose. The one is concerned with the 'how' of things whereas the other seeks to know the 'why'. And these things should at least cause us to pause for thought.

This is not an overtly religious book but an attempt to share values which may find acceptance with people holding a variety of views. Personally, I find in Christianity reason to believe and a satisfying faith but I recognise that many readers will not be in that position. They can be assured of my regard even as I hope that I may have theirs. But whatever our faith – or lack of it – the challenge to think is not one to be evaded by any of us. If believers sometimes doubt their faith it would be surprising if unbelievers did not sometimes doubt their doubts – and there may be very good reason for them to do so.

The Family

We need to give thought to the place of the family in these days. From time immemorial the family has been the basic building block of society. Is there now a danger that the traditional family unit will disintegrate and if so, what are the implications? To bring the matter closer to home perhaps we should give thought to our own family and what is happening to it. That could be tough but we should not put it into the 'too hard' basket.

Then, to widen the focus, we need to give thought to what is happening in our community. Do we like what we see? From the vantage point of one who has lived to reach retirement I would say that in many ways I appreciate the present age. More than most, I have seen the darker side of life but all is not doom and gloom – at least, not where I live. Enlightenment and humanity have a way of breaking through like shafts of sunlight on a cloudy day. Those who harp on about 'the good old days' probably have poor memories or wear rose-coloured spectacles for while some things about previous generations may have been good others were not so – like unrelieved poverty, infant mortality and the like.

Yet complacency would be inappropriate. If we give a thought to what is happening around us we will see problems that need to be addressed – such as unemployment, youth suicide and the like. We may duck the difficult issues by assuming that those are things for the 'pollies' to fix. In fact, the intractable problems in society call for the combined thought power – and consequent action – of a broad mass of people. If we don't give a thought it's hard to believe that we can give anything else.

One other point: the words 'think' and thank' may well be related. Certainly, if we *think* we will find reason to *thank*. Katherine Mansfield, the New Zealand writer, was convalescing in a beautiful spot high in the Alps when she exclaimed, "If only one could make some small grass-hoppery sound of praise to someone – *thanks to someone, but who?*"

The writer F. S. Smythe was in a happier position, lacking neither a necessary knowledge of a Benefactor nor a desire to give thanks. He recalled how one evening his party came to the Hildeseimer Hut in the Austrian Alps. Supper was ready, but before anyone sat down, staff and climbers gathered at the large picture window and 'thanks' were said. It seemed both simple and natural. He wrote, "High in the mountains in the regions tenanted by winds and storms, where life's necessities are procured at great cost, *men live thankfully*".

In more comfortable surroundings do we sometimes fail to thank because we fail to think? Consider the fact that before we have finished breakfast of a morning we may be indebted to half the world – a wheat farmer in Canada, a tea planter in Sri Lanka, a fruit grower in Australia. And then of course, there is the Source of "all things bright and beautiful".

~ 17 ~

Give Care

> Sometimes we can only see life's deeper
> hues through the prism of our tears.
>
> W.H.

The images of success which are generated in society may sometimes seem hard-nosed. For example, we envisage the tycoon ruthlessly bulldozing his way over anyone in his path and that may sometimes be just the way it is. But not always. In several countries I have had dealings with some of the wealthiest of people and have discovered that many of them have had 'soft centres' and genuine concern for the less fortunate. And so they should!

Unless it has a softer side success will be incomplete. Care giving is an essential element. Those who are wrapped up in themselves don't make very big parcels – whatever the size of their bank balances! Someone may have built a business – and that is good – but if he or she has not grown as a person then he or she can hardly be regarded as successful. And a capacity to show concern for others is a part of this. In many ways, those who count are those who care.

The word which may best describe what I have in mind has a slightly old-fashioned ring. It is compassion – and even as I write there comes into my mind the image of a little Albanian nun creeping among the sleeping poor in a Calcutta street. Mother Teresa has been pity personified and her example has stirred the world. But if she is destined to be regarded as a saint she has certainly not been the kind of person who could be described as "too heavenly minded to be any earthly use".

In his book, *Something Beautiful for God*, Malcolm Muggeridge wrote of Mother Teresa:

> *I have never met anyone less sentimental, less scatty, more down to earth... Pretty well everyone who has met her would agree, I think, that she is a unique person in the world today; not in our vulgar celebrity sense of having neon lighting about her head. Rather in the opposite sense – of someone who has merged herself in the common face of mankind and identified herself with human suffering and privation.*

With their inevitable stench, the poorer parts of Calcutta are places from which most westerners would choose to move out. Mother Teresa chose to move in and stay – for pity's sake. And her achievements give a different dimension to a word like 'success'. Sometimes we can only see life's deeper hues through the prism of our tears.

Real caring is more than a fuzzy feeling in the pit of the stomach or a passing flush of emotion. Real caring is costly. It not only means sharing other people's joys but weeping with those who weep – and the special significance of some people has been in their ability to do just that. So we could think of William Wilberforce agonising over the plight of slaves or Florence Nightingale concerned about the suffering of wounded soldiers.

William Blake put something of this – and more – into poetry when he wrote:

> *For a tear is an intellectual thing,*
> *And a sigh is the sword of an angel king,*
> *And the bitter groan of a martyr's woe*
> *Is an arrow from the Almighty's bow.*

Rabbi Bluoch was a Jewish padre in the First World War but apparently, in the units of the French Army with which he served, there were not many Jews – most of the troops being, at least nominally, Roman Catholics. So when he went out into no man's land the Rabbi took a crucifix with him. And it was while he was holding the Cross before a dying soldier that a fatal bullet drilled him through.

For Pity's Sake?

Aristotle seems to have regarded pity as a troublesome emotion to be purged harmlessly out of the system through watching tragic drama! That may or may not be a misrepresentation of what Aristotle really meant but certainly, many of the great humanitarian institutions in the world – hospitals, leper colonies and the like – owe their origin to people whose pity led not merely to harmless purging of emotions in a theatre but to positive action and who cared enough to do something for the sick or otherwise needy.

There are still many people who are ready to give time and effort and resources to help those in need and in the several countries where I have worked I have been inspired by such folk. In Canada I had a seat on the boards of no fewer than 11 hospitals across the country and got to appreciate the tireless efforts of literally thousands of volunteers. They served in all kinds of ways without looking for recognition or reward. *And they were happy and fulfilled in doing so*. It has been said that there are some people who know the price of everything and the value of nothing but the reverse is the case with others who give of themselves and who are the salt of the earth.

In his *Life of John Bright*, G. M. Trevelyan tells a story about Jacob Bright, John's father. One day he was coming up the hill from town to his home and found a neighbour in great trouble on the road. His horse had met with an accident and it had been necessary to kill it. People were crowding around the man saying how sorry they were. To one man who kept repeating this most loudly Jacob Bright said, "I am sorry five pounds. How much are you sorry?" Then he passed around the hat for money to buy the unfortunate fellow another horse.

Compassion may well lead us to *do something* after we've said "I'm sorry!" The challenge is to give whatever may be possible in terms of time, effort or resources. In a home for needy girls in Fiji I saw a notice which declared, "Others will not care how much we know until they know how much we care." That would be a fair comment.

~ 18 ~

Give Motivation

> *Few things are more satisfying than being able to inspire other human beings to accept new challenges.*
>
> W.H.

*H*ow to get people fired up is the challenge which faces all leaders and how to stir people and dispel apathy is sometimes a problem. Yet the folk who may seem to lack motivation in one department of life (their work, for example) may be highly motivated in other ways.

I think of the by no means isolated instance of a young man I will call Des. Married and with a young family, he had either been unemployed or in poorly-paid jobs. Yet when offered a perfectly viable and ethical business opportunity that would have supplemented his limited income and even surpassed it he said that he didn't have time. Pressed a little, he listed the various leisure activities which filled most of his spare moments and to which he gave priority rating. Of course, the choice was his and I respected that, although I found his decision a little strange.

So how can people be motivated in new ways? What buttons must be pressed?

The answer can hardly be contained in a 'one-liner', as everyone is different, and it all depends on many things. But one thing may be fairly obvious. *If we are to give motivation we must*

71

first be motivated ourselves. After all, we can't give what we haven't got. And the people around us will soon know whether, and to what extent, *we* are motivated.

The perceptiveness of ordinary people should never be underestimated. They will soon know whether the boss is a hack, an uninspired functionary, or personally sold on the mission of the organisation. It will be apparent not so much in official pronouncements as in chance remarks and unconscious reactions.

Motivation is in the mind. It has to do with attitude – and this is where a leader needs to be out in front, convinced and confident. An anonymous writer has penned the following lines:

> *If you think you're beaten, you are.*
> *If you think you daren't, you don't.*
> *If you'd like to win but think you can't.*
> *It's almost certain you won't ...*
>
> *... sooner or later the person who wins*
> *Is the person who thinks he (she) can.*

Thus confidence is important and so is character. St Augustine said, "What I live by I impart". He also said, "One loving spirit sets another heart on fire." If our dream is big enough it will be something we want others to share. Our enthusiasm will prove contagious – whether it be for a community project, the building up of a business or whatever. Motivation is more likely to be caught than taught.

We often make the mistake of thinking that our influence must almost entirely depend upon our ability to 'talk the talk' but that may not be the case. In his book, *Silent Messages*, Dr Albert Mehrebian claimed that 55 per cent of the messages we receive come through physiology (body language?), 38 per cent through voice (tone and inflection?) and only 7 per cent through words.

By whatever means, leaders need to share their vision. They need to help other people to dream dreams which will inspire them to go many extra miles to make them come true. They may also need to motivate others to set themselves goals which are, to use an acronym, Specific, Measurable, Attainable, Relevant and Time-framed. That is being SMART, but how can it be done?

Gone Fishing

At one time I had oversight of some community programs in the Pacific kingdom of Tonga. Many Tongan men were going to work in New Zealand or Australia and in some cases that was not helping family life. We therefore set up a project with the aim of motivating and providing those ready to work with the means both to stay with their families and support them. With overseas aid we had fishing boats built and then men paid a small maintenance fee for the privilege of going out in the boats and keeping and selling all the fish that they could catch. For them that meant financial independence and a considerable achievement.

In Australia a millionaire friend of mine was supportive of a project for homeless and unemployed young people. It involved a certain amount of building work. My friend could have written a cheque and felt that he had done his part but in fact he did more. He travelled a long distance, rolled up his sleeves and 'got stuck in' helping the young people refurbish a centre made available to them. As he worked alongside them he inspired those youngsters with the idea that they too could one day 'make it big'.

In New Zealand I was involved in the administration of numerous employment programs. Our concern was for people who may have been so caught in the cycle of dependency that they had lost the will to work. Their dull eyes said it all. Hope was dead. Then under skilled supervision they discovered that they had latent abilities for which there could be a market. For some of those long-term unemployed what seemed an impossible dream became a fact of life. They were 'no-hopers' no longer.

For some the dream may be freedom from the treadmill of repetitive employment and the opportunity of running their own business. They know that the commercial highway is littered with casualties but still they dream and I know a number who, with suitable coaching, are defying all the odds and succeeding. The entrepreneurial spirit is not dead but it needs encouraging.

Some people will not be motivated by the thought of material gain. For example, they may already have made their money and, regardless of the level of remuneration, be looking for a satisfying second career working with people – in the ministry or in social service, for example. I have had the opportunity of talking with many such people and have encouraged them to lift their sights and follow their dream. To be without motivation is to be an obstacle to others – like a car which has run out of gasoline! But few things are more satisfying than being able to inspire other human beings to accept new challenges.

Being only human, those who seek to give inspiration and motivation to others will sometimes have their own fears and uncertainties. But for the sake of those who look to them as well as for their own sake they will press on, facing their fears but not being controlled by them. They may take on board the words of a whimsical little song from *The King and I* by Rogers and Hammerstein:

> *Whenever I feel afraid*
> *I hold my head erect*
> *And whistle a happy tune*
> *So no one will suspect*
> *I'm afraid ...*
> *The result of this deception*
> *Is very strange to tell*
> *For when I fool the people I fear*
> *I fool myself as well.*

~ 19 ~

Give Team Support

> *No man is an island.*
>
> John Donne

*T*emperamentally, we are all different. For example, we may be 'morning people' or we may be 'night people' – 'fowls' or 'owls'! We may be volatile and 'quick response' folk or we may be of the stolid, 'steady-as-she-goes' kind. Some are naturally team players while others are loners. But despite our differences, chances are that we will have to work together and failure to do so may be disastrous.

There is a joke about two shipwrecked sailors sitting in the back of a lifeboat doing nothing while people at the front of the boat were bailing furiously. One said to the other, "Thank goodness that hole isn't at *our* end of the boat!" Far-fetched? Maybe – but not so far from the attitude we may sometimes encounter. Yet as another joker has put it, "If we don't hang together we'll hang separately."

To some extent we will often be brought together willy-nilly, whether we wish it or not. For example, people are thrown together at the check-out of a supermarket although they may have little in common except a desire to get to their cars. Such folk may form a group but they do not constitute a team and in this chapter it is team building that I want to consider.

So what makes the difference? Robyn Keal has defined a team as a "group of two or more people working cooperatively together, sharing a common purpose, vision, values and resources". The same writer has the acronym, Together Everyone Achieves More – with which we may all agree in principle but sometimes find difficult in practice.

Team building may involve giving and giving up. If it calls for a maximum contribution from every member it may also require the sacrifice of unilateral action and the right to call the shots regardless of what others may think. Yet the old adage is usually true: two (or more) heads are likely to be better than one. Team spirit can produce a synergy – that is, an effect that exceeds the sum of individual effects. Two plus two may equal five!

Sometimes we may have the chance to choose a team. Getting the right balance of talent and temperament will be important. We may long for a 'dream team' but may have to come to terms with the 'possible and the available'. We may also conclude that a team of people with modest talent who can work together may be more effective than a group of stars all intent on doing their own thing.

Sometimes the choice of team will not be ours. We will have to work with what is given and the challenge will be to make the best use of the team we have rather than denigrate it and pine for the impossible. It has been said that when the going gets tough the tough will get going and the test of working together under difficulty may well be part of the challenge.

An essential of good team work is mutual respect. On New Year's Day 1998, Peter Treseder, Keith Williams and Ian Brown became the first Australians to walk unassisted to the South Pole. They spent 60 days crossing 1,400 km of ice and snow through blizzards of up to 160 km an hour, each pulling a sled full of provisions.

Frostbite and a twisted ankle nearly forced Brown and Williams to quit but eventually they made it. When they arrived back in Australia Treseder said, "We have had some tough times as a team before. Occasionally things will erupt into a bit of an argument. But underlying it all is this deep respect that each of us has for the other, so that I am sure that we have come out of this trip better friends than we went into it. And that is tremendous."

Common Aim

Giving team support will mean remaining focused on common aims. Personal agendas there may be, but they must not override the shared objective. The team and its task is most important. Then *care* for other team members will be vital. After all they are not cogs in a machine but people who need to be treated as such. For that reason good *communication* must be maintained.

A survey of employees by the Padgett Thompson organisation in the USA sought to establish what things they valued most. Among many items the top three were: appreciation for a job well done; a feeling that they were 'in' on things; and management's understanding of their personal problems. Significantly, they were not the things which supervisors thought employees would value most which suggests that perhaps communication left something to be desired.

Years ago I was given the oversight of a dozen centres of work in the county of Devon, England while having direct responsibility for operations in the main city of Exeter. The dual role was interesting, to say the least. I had a team of about twenty leaders and I quickly realised that they were the key to the situation.

Once a month we met for a day of study, discussion and 'combined operations' when we sought to stimulate each other. Sometimes I would speak of a project which we were initiating in Exeter and encourage others to follow suit. At other times the initiative might come from another quarter, which was fine. Everybody was encouraged to pass on ideas and if someone was ready to pick one up and run with it they were applauded and supported in every way possible. I recall those days as being very busy but incredibly rewarding because of the fine team spirit.

In sporting circles the importance of a coach is well recognised and in other fields the role of the team leader will also be vital. The aim must not only be to see growth in the business, enterprise, or whatever, but growth in the people conducting it. The continued expansion of the one may well depend on the development of the other.

Good team leaders will seek to set the pace. In cricket reference is sometimes made to a 'captain's innings' – a batting performance to inspire team mates and stiffen the resolve to win. That can make all the difference. If leaders don't lead how can others be expected to follow?

But the leader may sometimes need to facilitate the efforts of others rather than do the things himself (or herself). To make a point it may sometimes be necessary to overstate it. I am sure that Mark Twain was doing that and had his tongue in his cheek when he wrote, "Never learn to do anything. If you don't learn you will always find someone else to do it for you."

A Difference

There is a world of difference between a dysfunctional group and an effective team. A situation where everybody does their own thing is unlikely to be productive but cooperation can work wonders.

Many years ago I used to teach students in a particular subject at the Royal Military School of Music in England. Immediately before the scheduled time for my session was a period when all musicians could do their own thing. Whether they were players of brass or woodwind or other instruments, they could practise as they saw fit. So sometimes, as I entered the gates of the school, the sound was more suggestive of bedlam than of a training centre for professional musicians. The noise was awful! Yet once a week those same musicians would give a concert of superb music under the baton of the director of music. What made the difference? It was an acceptance of authority and a disciplined working together in the pursuit of excellence. That was team work – and it was good.

Lessons in team work may come from unexpected quarters. When I was living in Canada I was sometimes fascinated to see a flock of large wild geese flying in perfect formation. I had sometimes thought of geese as being of low intelligence for why else would a foolish person be described as a 'silly goose'? But I have had second thoughts in the light of the following facts included in a presentation by Angeles Arrien based on the work of Milton Olson and quoted in *On Great Service* by Leonard L. Berry.

As each goose flaps its wings it creates an 'uplift' for the birds that follow. By flying in 'V' formation, the whole flock adds 71% greater flying range than if each bird flew alone. When a goose falls out of formation, it suddenly feels the drag and resistance of flying alone. It quickly moves back into formation to take advantage of the lifting power of the bird immediately in front of it.

When the lead goose tires, it rotates back into the formation, and another goose flies to the point position. The geese flying in formation honk to encourage those up front to keep up their speed. When a goose gets sick, wounded or shot down, two geese drop out of formation and follow it down to help and protect it. They stay with it until it is either able to fly or dies. Then they launch out with another formation or catch up with the flock.

It seems that human beings could learn a lot about team work, mutual support and solidarity by watching those not-so-silly geese!

~ 20 ~

Give Money

> *There was a man*
> *Some called him mad;*
> *The more he gave*
> *The more he had.*
>
> John Bunyan

*T*he area near the pocket may be the most sensitive part of a person's anatomy! Certainly, people can get very 'twitchy' if you get too near what an American friend of mine calls 'the hip pocket nerve'. This book spells out that there are many ways in which we can give. Money isn't everything – but as a rule, we can't get very far without it. So we'd better give the matter some thought.

As a practical utility for commercial purposes the value of money is obvious. In less sophisticated societies trade was – and sometimes still is – by barter, where giving must be in kind rather than cash.

(I received a report from a part of Africa where people still bring a handful of maize or a young chicken for the church collection. One worshipper brought a goat which, appropriately enough, was tethered to the treasurer's leg during the service. Unfortunately, at a critical moment the animal decided to bolt with the worthy treasurer hopping behind it – a case of the collection running away with the treasurer!)

There was a report of a limited barter system operating among welfare recipients in a modern western society with vegetables being given for services rendered and so on. But clearly that would not be practical on a wide scale. Imagine taking a lusty young cockerel to the supermarket for the purpose of payment instead of the house-keeping purse or credit card!

Money is a convenience and a necessary one. In itself it has no moral significance but what people do to get it and how they use it may well have ethical connotations. Francis Bacon was perhaps overly negative when he wrote, "Of great riches there is no real use, except it be in the distribution; the rest is but conceit."

Money *can* bring many benefits and most people don't need convincing on that point! But money may cost too much if people are unscrupulous about the way they get it or selfish in the way they use it. Mother Teresa said, "God has given us things not to hold but to use and share". There may be nothing wrong about making money but it does bring the need for responsibility.

We need to be *responsible* in our giving of money whether it be to a church or a charity or needy individuals. Strange as it may sound, it is possible to be irresponsibly generous! We can give in such a way that we pauperise people. Our giving can be a substitute for self-help instead of a stimulus for it. There are times when we *should* send food to people in stricken areas of the world but it is good if we then can go on to help those people support themselves. In the long run, a hand up is better than a hand out. As a Chinese proverb puts it, "If you give a man a fish you feed him for a day but if you teach him how to fish you feed him for a lifetime".

Without being tardy, it is right that donors – be they individual, corporate or governmental – and charitable agencies should seek to be responsible in the distribution of aid. That is part of good stewardship.

Proportionate Giving

Then it is right that our giving should be *in proportion* to our resources. For a billionaire a donation of $100 might be little more than small change but for a widowed pensioner it might mean giving out of sacrifice rather than out of surplus. Unfortunately, when it comes to giving some people will stop at nothing!

Years ago, in America, a young lad from a very poor home went to work for a company in New York. His devout mother told him that for every dollar he earned he ought to give 10 cents to the church or to charity. He worked hard and as the firm expanded he climbed the ladder of success until he became a partner and then the sole owner of the business. He continued to give away a tenth of his income.

As he grew rich he was able to give two tenths, then four tenths, then half his income. Eventually, having educated his family and made proper provision for them, he was able to live on the interest of his wealth and give everything else to worthy causes. By the way, we may well see the man's name when we go into our bathroom. He was William Colgate, the manufacturer of soaps and toothpaste.

Another man of great wealth was Andrew Carnegie. A poor emigrant from Scotland to the United States, he rose from being a bobbin boy in a cotton factory to being a steel producer at a time of great demand. In 1889 he wrote an essay, *The Gospel of Wealth*, in which he formulated his belief that it was the duty of the rich to distribute their surplus wealth. In 1900 he began to set up a vast number of charitable foundations to support education, research and world peace and really set a pattern for other philanthropists.

A modern benefactor would be the well-known Australian Dick Smith, a wealthy businessman and entrepreneur to whom many people have cause to be grateful. As an example, Pat Daley, a headquarters spokesman for The Salvation Army in Sydney, informed me that a few years ago *The Daily Telegraph* carried a report of a two million dollar shortfall in the Army's annual appeal. Dick Smith read the report and made up the shortfall. The following year he was present at a meeting when a young Salvationist spoke of her work in one of the Army's refuges for abused women. Dick was deeply moved and suggested that all present should double whatever they had given previously and he set an example by donating a further four million dollars!

For most of us any giving of money must be on a very much smaller scale! However, even with our more limited resources we can learn how rewarding giving can be. Of course, we shouldn't give *in order* to gain (that would be unworthy) but there is no doubt that those who are generous do gain, sometimes financially, but always in some way.

I would suggest that our giving should not be spasmodic but *regular* and *systematic*. Those charged with the heavy responsibility of administering charitable funds are grateful for gifts of all kinds but are particularly appreciative of those who give consistent support and who therefore make responsible budgeting much easier. Some governments encourage giving to charities by making tax allowances under certain conditions. That is not unreasonable, bearing in mind that charities often relieve some of what would otherwise be pressure on the public purse to provide for the needy.

Then our giving should not be done reluctantly but *gladly* and *gratefully*. St Augustine said that we should pray for miracles and work for results and if our prayers have been answered and our work has been rewarded then we should show our gratitude by sharing with those less fortunate. The Bible declares that God loves the *cheerful* giver and the original Greek word translated as cheerful is *hilaron*, from which we also get the word hilarious. It might be said that there is special blessing for 'hilarious givers' – and they are sometimes few and far between!

Thomas Carlisle told how, when he was a boy, a beggar came to the door when he was alone in the house. On a boyish impulse he went to the receptacle containing his own savings and gave the beggar everything that was in it. He declared that at no other time had he known such happiness as that which came to him in that moment.

Some of the most joyous people I have known have been those who have mastered the art of giving. They may have had only modest means but they have given out of what they had. Others have been very wealthy but have had the same attitude. (The principles of giving hold regardless of the amounts involved. It is said that the Almighty doesn't only look at what we give but at what we have left!)

Many will feel that one of the reasons for wanting to make money is to be able to do some good with it. Fair enough.

~ 21 ~

Give Appreciation

> *The way to develop the best that is in a man is by appreciation and encouragement.*
>
> Charles Schwab

*A*ny leader worth his salt must sometimes take people to task on some issue. There are those who find this difficult and either do nothing, refer the matter to headquarters or otherwise ignore dealing with the issue directly. Yet, for the good of the business or organisation, dereliction of duty or declining standards must be addressed and it is a mistaken 'kindness' and a palpable weakness which refuses to say or do what is required.

However, it is usually possible to express praise as well as criticism so that to some extent the one helps to balance the other and indicates how the future can be more positive than the past. But strangely, if some find it difficult to offer even constructive criticism others apparently find it as hard to express appreciation. The words 'thank you' seem to die on their pursed lips. Even a faint smile of appreciation is hard to come by!

I think of a private secretary who was not only extremely competent but ready and willing to work late or do almost anything that was required. She had a new boss who was not only irascible but apparently found it hard to express appreciation for anything, which was a great pity for it left a valuable staff member very discouraged.

A small book with a large circulation is *The One Minute Manager* by Kenneth Blanchard and Spencer Johnson. Following is some of the advice it provides:

The one minute reprimand works well when you:

1. Tell people beforehand that you are going to let them know how they are doing and in no uncertain terms.

The first half of the reprimand:

2. Reprimand people immediately.

3. Tell people what they did wrong – be specific.

4. Tell people how you feel about what they did wrong – and in no uncertain terms.

5. Stop for a few seconds of uncomfortable silence to let them feel how you feel.

The second half of the reprimand:

6. Shake hands, or touch them in a way that lets them know that you are honestly on their side.

7. Remind them how much you value them.

8. Reaffirm that you think well of them but not of their performance in this situation.

9. Realise that when the reprimand is over, it's over.

Reprimands wrapped in appreciation are usually not too hard to accept. In the same book from which I have quoted is the suggestion that managers should try to catch people doing something *correctly* and affirm them accordingly.

Our American cousins may do more with expressions of appreciation than folk in other countries. They go in for plaques and appreciation lunches and the like. I have heard tell of a wall of thanks where, anonymously or not, people could put notes of appreciation for service beyond the call of duty. Recognition of extra effort may be given in an in-house magazine or newsletter or the service can be mentioned in a staff meeting. While criticism should almost invariably be given privately appreciation should sometimes be given publicly, and it can often mean a lot.

At some time in their lives, most people have laboured under the impression that their work has not been recognised or appreciated. What they have needed may have been no big deal, just some affirmation which may have cost little but meant much.

I heard about some church youth group members who decided to give their minister a surprise by putting on a special meal. When he asked the reason they said, "When you came there was a great welcome and you had a good kick off. When you go you will probably have a good send off. We just thought that you could do with a kick in the interim!" I am sure that the gesture would have meant a lot.

A colleague of Lord Grey's described how he dealt with a difficult patch. He said, "I was feeling depressed this morning and so I went to see Grey. I wanted to be made to feel two inches taller." Don't we all know the feeling?

Even people in positions of authority may sometimes need to be affirmed, but in some cultures there is such a fear of appearing obsequious or fawning that subordinates remain tight-lipped when, without any question of being manipulative, a sincere word of appreciation would be helpful.

An Attitude of Gratitude

Top executives are commonly paid astronomical salaries in these days, but consider the case of Charles Schwab. When money values were very different from what they are today, he was paid a million dollars a year by Andrew Carnegie, the Scottish steel magnate who made his fortune in the United States during the last century.

Schwab didn't attract such a salary because he knew more about the manufacture of steel than plenty of other people. He confessed that he had many employees more knowledgeable than he was. Then, as Dale Carnegie records in *How to Win Friends and Influence People*, he indicated the secret of his success.

I consider my ability to arouse enthusiasm among the men the greatest asset I possess, and the way to develop the best that is in a man is by appreciation and encouragement.

There is nothing else that so kills the ambitions of a man as criticisms from his superiors. I never criticise anyone. I believe in giving a man incentive to work. So I am anxious to praise but loathe to find fault. If I like anything, I am hearty in my approbation and lavish in my praise...

In my wide association in life, meeting with many and great men in various parts of the world I have yet to find the man, however great and exalted his station who did not do better work and put forth greater effort under the spirit of approval than he would ever do under the spirit of criticism.

I would question Schwab's policy of *never* criticising anyone. Taken literally that may be going too far. But Schwab obviously discovered that praise pays. Moreover, he knew that sincere appreciation could make life worth living for battlers and bosses alike. He said that therein was the secret of his one-time boss, Andrew Carnegie, who sought to praise his colleagues even in the epitaph he composed for his own tombstone. It read, "Here lies one who knew how to get around him men who were cleverer than himself".

An attitude of gratitude can work wonders. Simply giving appreciation may be one of the secrets of success.

~ 22 ~

Give Loyalty

> *Loyalty is the glue that holds a community together.*
>
> W.H.

*L*oyalty – like motherhood – is universally praised and appreciated but not always easy to work out. We need to think about it in a contemporary context but first we may pause to recall two historical examples of men who inspired intense loyalty.

In July 1746 a huge reward was offered for the capture of Charles Edward Stuart, 'Bonnie Prince Charlie' – one of the most romantic figures in Scottish history. As a hungry fugitive he sought shelter in a hut in Glen Morriston where eight men lived together, themselves outlaws and doubtless on short rations. They knew the stranger's identity and had only to lift a finger to earn the money yet instead they risked their lives to go into Fort Augustus to buy a piece of gingerbread as a present for the prince they would not betray. That didn't make sense – or did it?

There was a time when there was disaffection and threatened mutiny among Napoleon's Guards. The Emperor sat alone in a little room in his palace, a room which was in between two large apartments. The members of the Guard were assembled in one apartment. Each man was summoned in turn, and as he entered the small room the door was shut. Not a word was spoken but

Napoleon clasped his hand and looked him full in the face and then the man went out into the other apartment. And when all had passed through, one by one, the disaffection was over and loyalty was restored. The personal touch had made the difference.

But what price loyalty today in what sometimes seems to be a very impersonal society? Has it gone by the board? Is it a luxury that we can afford? Is it something we can afford not to have? Isn't it the glue that holds a community together?

Looking back over the years I have good reason to be grateful for the loyalty of colleagues, friends and voluntary helpers who have not only been supportive to me personally but have joined me in common causes and in ways which have sometimes been costly. They confirm my belief that loyalty is still alive and well in many quarters.

In *The Loyalty Link* Dennis G. McCarthy claims that in business employee loyalty and customer loyalty usually go together. His research leads him to say that companies with high customer satisfaction and retention usually have a high level of employee satisfaction, low staff turnover and high efficiency, while the opposite is also true.

He claims that the secret of ensuring customer loyalty is to nurture loyal staff who will make discretionary efforts, over and above what may be required, in order to exceed customers' expectations. Customers who are merely not dissatisfied will be very unpredictable and liable to take their custom elsewhere. But those who have been surprised by 'extra mile' service will develop a loyalty which will bring them back again and again.

Let me tell you about Margaret. She works for a local supplier and her firm was unable to fulfil an order for me at the promised time, despite her considerable efforts and due to deplorable tardiness on the part of the wholesalers. I was not pleased but I was impressed by the lengths to which Margaret went in order to meet my need and her obvious concern. Because of her care I will probably continue to deal with her firm, whereas I might not have done if I had been treated in an offhand manner.

So customer retention may well depend on employees who are loyal, not merely in that they front up on time and do what is required of them, but in that they are 'people people' and have a genuine interest in satisfying those they seek to serve. Such employees may be worth more than money in the bank. They should be looked after not only in financial terms but with the creative consideration that makes a work situation a good place to be. Loyalty should be a two-way street.

Conflicts of Loyalty

Sometimes conflicts of loyalties arise and there may be no easy answers. That can be true in life at large and not least in the commercial world. Automation can be both a boon and a bane. Machines can do the work of men and women but what about the employees who are sacrificed on the altar of progress? It is said that in order to survive firms must be mean and lean. Downsizing – a euphemism for sacking people – may be seen as the only option. That's tough for those who feel a loyalty to shareholders, customers and employees alike. Can humanity and efficiency be reconciled? The effort will certainly be made by an administration with a human face but it is no good pretending that it will always be easy.

Conflicts may come in other ways. It may sometimes be necessary to decide whether loyalty to one's immediate boss or loyalty to the company or to one's colleagues should be given precedence. An employee may sometimes face the dilemma as to whether because of a larger loyalty he should 'blow the whistle' on a colleague engaged in unethical practices or whether 'mateship' should preclude this.

Then working out the balance of loyalties between our work and our family may present problems. To some extent the family may share in the fruit of our 'success' but how high a price can we expect them to pay for it in terms of our absence from home, for example?

We should be loyal to our family. As the saying goes, "Blood is thicker than water." In some cultures family allegiance overrides everything else. I have known people in some parts of the world who have felt completely justified in giving away something on the request of a relative – even if it wasn't their property to give! We may rightly think that this is taking things too far, but certainly we all owe a debt of loyalty to family and friends and most decent folk would want to honour that.

We all have to work out our hierarchy of loyalties. Not all choices are between black and white. Often they are between varying shades of grey and people can spend nights tossing and turning and wondering just what to do.

Perhaps the first thing to be said is that we have to be true to ourselves – loyal to the royal within us, we might say. We can't afford to sell out on our core values. After all, at the end of the day we've got to be able to live with ourselves. Shakespeare put it well when he wrote: "This above all: to thine own self be true, And it must follow, as the night the day, Thou canst not then be false to any man". Having thoughtfully balanced our loyalties and sought guidance – human and divine – we can only do what seems best, and leave the rest.

In one sense loyalty cannot be bought; but it can be deserved. It can find expression in small things as well as large. Through all the complexities of life we should seek to give loyalty, and that will enhance the quality of such success as may come our way.

~ 23 ~

Give It A Go

> *If there is fruit on the branches we may*
> *have to go out on a limb to get it.*
>
> W.H.

About the middle of the nineteenth century a great uncle of
mine decided to leave his home in the country town of
Axbridge, Somerset, in England and set sail for Australia. The
young man must have struck it rich in Perth, because his parents,
accompanied by the rest of their children (including my
grandmother), decided to sell up, lock stock and barrel, and join
him. Unfortunately, their ship struck a rock and sank not long after
they left Plymouth. They lost everything except their lives and
settled in Wales. Three generations later I came to Australia in
connection with my work and later decided to retire here where
some of my own family had settled.

What eventually happened to Great Uncle Swearse I don't
know, but he was one of many who, like the Biblical Abraham,
'went out not knowing whither he went'. They were entrepreneurs,
pioneers who helped to make Australia what it is. Some of their
kith and kin also sought a new life in the USA, Canada or New
Zealand. They decided to 'give it a go', to use an Aussie phrase

which seems to sum up the spirit of the pioneers, and many of their descendants have cause to be grateful to them.

The question is: what about us? As generations have passed has the dynamism of the pioneers tended to run down? Has *our* get up and go got up and gone? Or does something of the entrepreneurial spirit remain in us? Our success or failure may well depend upon the answer.

It seems to me that the entrepreneurial spirit will contain certain elements which we need to have in order to be successful. First, I would mention *hope* which is to the spirit what oxygen is to the body. Hope makes what is potential and in the future, present, actual and dynamic in our thinking.

When Alexander the Great crossed into Asia he gave away most of his possessions and was asked, "What will you keep for yourself?" "I keep hope," he replied. The entrepreneur needs to be buoyed by hope, for there will be times when the going will be hard and disappointments come one after another. As former Australian Prime Minister Malcolm Fraser is reported to have said, "Life wasn't meant to be easy." It certainly won't always be easy for those who are ahead of the pack, having a go when all around them people are giving up the ghost.

Almost by definition, the entrepreneurial spirit implies a willingness to *take risks*. Thomas Aquinas said, "If the primary vision of a captain were to preserve his ship he would never leave port." Anyone can be smart with hindsight but those who launch out in new ways need foresight, and that will be a less certain indicator. Prudent judgement may lead to the conclusion that doing nothing may also carry risks; the status quo may not be an attractive option and having the courage to try something new may be the best case scenario. If there is fruit on the branches we may have to go out on a limb to get it!

I saw the following statement on someone's t-shirt: "If you're not living on the edge you're taking up too much room." That may mean different things for different people. To my mind it suggested the need to be willing to take some risks, calculated and cautious perhaps, but courageous nonetheless.

Energy

Then the entrepreneur will need an abundance of *enthusiasm and energy*. Let those who will despise small beginnings. As the saying goes: a journey of a thousand miles begins with a single step. A great business may begin with one small sale. In 1882 Michael Marks, a Jewish refugee from what was then Russian Poland, arrived in England and with a tray around his neck started selling haberdashery in villages around Leeds in Yorkshire, England. In 1884 he borrowed five pounds from a wholesaler named Isaac Dewhirst and before the end of the year was able to take a stall in Leeds open-air market. He could not read or write English and so he put up a notice which read, "Don't ask the price, it's a penny." Dewhirst's cashier, Tom Spencer, became a partner.

Today, Marks and Spencer is the name of a large and respected chain of stores in Britain. What began by turning over pennies now turns over pounds by the million. But getting things rolling from a standing start would have taken some doing. The two intrepid pioneers shouting their wares in a cold Yorkshire market could never have guessed where their efforts would lead but doubtless it was enthusiasm and energy which got them started and kept them going – and thousands of employees and customers have reason to be grateful to them.

Many people live with the vain hope that success will just happen for them. Wiser souls make up their minds that they will *make it happen* through their initiative and hard work.

In a rapidly changing world the entrepreneur will need to *adapt and adopt new methods* to cope with new demands. What worked in the age of the horse and buggy may be totally inappropriate in the era of computer science. Principles don't change but methods must and one of the marks of the entrepreneur is a willingness to try new approaches.

It has been said that if at first we don't succeed we're running about normal! We have to try again or try a different approach. In science some of the most important discoveries haven't come with the first experiment, or even the hundred and first – and it is likewise in the realm of business. Success stories in real life have often had a few false starts. These may not be trumpeted but they are par for the course.

The challenge to 'give it a go' may be something we should accept not only for our own sake but for the sake of those who will come after us. When I lived in Canada I had contact with many people engaged in English as a Second Language courses. Many of them were refugees and had lived under intolerable regimes. Their determination was not only to improve their own lot but that of their children as well.

I have met other people who have launched out in business or in some other way because of a desire that their families would have a better start in life than they had. That sounds fair enough. I guess that we'll never know whether or not we can succeed unless we 'give it a go'.

~ 24 ~

Give A Boost

> *I am but one, but I am one.*
> *I cannot do everything, but I can do something.*
> *What I can do, I ought to do,*
> *What I ought to do,*
> *God helping me, I will do.*
>
> Anon.

I read about a man who bought a piece of land near a roundabout at an intersection on one of the main arterial roads leading out of London, England. He planned to develop the land as a nursery and grow flowers and plants of one kind and another but somehow, whatever he did, little would grow. Eventually he took samples of the soil to an agricultural chemist. They were analysed and the discovery was made that they contained a tremendous amount of iron.

Enquiries were made in the district and it was discovered that before the arterial road was built local villagers had used the plot of land as a dumping ground for their old tin cans, saucepans, tin baths and the like. The rains had descended, the floods had come and great had been the rust thereof! Only when it was expertly treated could the land produce crops again.

It struck me that this was a kind of modern parable. So much has been dumped on the soil of society and upon some of our individual lives. There may have been unemployment, violence, child abuse and much, much more. Is that one reason why our lives are not as fruitful as they might be? Maybe yes, maybe no.

T. S. Eliot, one of the greatest of modern English poets, has written:

> *The desert is not remote in southern tropics*
> *The desert is not only around the corner;*
> *The desert is squeezed into the tube train next to you,*
> *The desert is in the heart of your brother.*

Some of the poison in the soul of society has gone deep. The problem is profound and may call for social and psychological remedies. Certainly, I believe in the need for spiritual renewal. The heart of the human problem is the problem of the human heart and those elements in human nature which, writ large, constitute the problems of society such as war, oppression and the like. But all is not lost and our greatest success may be in boosting the confidence of those who may think that it is.

For some people, part of their problem may be a low sense of self-worth. Negative ideas may have been dumped on them from an early age and they will have added to the rubbish themselves. In consequence, they haven't grown as persons and their lives haven't proved to be as fruitful as they would have wished.

In his book, *See You at the Top,* Zig Ziglar outlines some of the manifestations of a poor self-image. They include: jealousy without cause; an over-reaction to criticism or teasing; lack of motivation; and an undue emphasis on material possessions to the exclusion of other values.

We need to realise that nobody is a nobody; everybody is a somebody. Although the colloquial term 'junkie' may be in a dictionary to describe a drug addict, no one is a junk male – or female, come to that – although some have taken in 'junk' and suffered as a result. People may feel that they are on the scrap heap but they can recycled – or be redeemed, to use a more traditional term. Every person matters and we can boost our own growth and that of others by repeating that truth over and over again.

Ziglar writes of a Dallas businesswoman named Mary Crowley who said:

> *You are somebody because God doesn't take time to make a nobody and once you learn how much you matter to God, you don't have to go out and show the world how much you matter.*

Then, with a twinkle in her eye she added, "God made man, took one look and said, 'I can do better than that' – and made woman." With difficulty, I resist the temptation to comment on her last remark!

Born to Win

We may have been conditioned for failure but we were born to win and we should not allow anyone to steal that realisation from us. Especially, we shouldn't steal it from ourselves. When we were conceived we beat about five hundred thousand competitors. From infancy we have thrown off innumerable challenges from germs and other kinds of elements. We were built to win and encourage others to win.

As distinct from other forms of life, we have the capacity to choose our destiny. We can grow if we want to grow. Instead of languishing with a 'poor me' syndrome or blaming our circumstances we can be affirmed ourselves and affirm others. Then instead of being part of the problem we will be part of the answer. Now I am certainly not suggesting that we should be conceited or *puffed up* but that we should be *built up* by accepting the truth that we are all unique and of infinite worth. If we could really get that into our heads it could transform our relationship with ourselves and with other people. With some divine and human help we can be what we were meant to be.

Sometimes we hear of people receiving compensation of many thousands of dollars for the loss of an eye or a leg in an accident. Would we change places with such folk? Surely not! Our limbs and our faculties are too valuable for us to want to lose them. And we are more than the sum of our various parts. So what's all this nonsense about being of little worth? With all the wonders of computer technology the human mind is still more wonderful – as the creator is greater than the created. We all have powers of thought which may be very much underused. Instead of belittling what has been given to us we should seek to realise our potential for growth.

Other people often take us at our own valuation. If we are prone to put ourselves down or write ourselves off then we can hardly blame others if they take a similar view of us. We don't have to try and compensate for our low esteem by bluff or bluster. We can quietly realise the worth which is our birthright and give encouragement and affirmation to other people to believe for themselves.

The novelist A. J. Cronin told of a district nurse he knew when he was working as a doctor. For 20 years she had served single-handed in a district ten miles long. He said:

> *I marvelled at her patience, her fortitude and her cheerfulness. She was never too tired at night to rise for an urgent call. Her salary was most inadequate and late one night, after a particularly strenuous day, I ventured to protest to her, "Nurse, why don't you make them pay you more? God knows you are worth it." She replied, "If God knows that I am worth it that's all that matters to me."*

We must not allow the poison of negative thinking about ourselves or other people to get into our system. We are all worth a whole heap and if we can share that perception we may be more successful than we realise and provide a boost for ourselves and others as well.

~ 25 ~

Give And Take

> *There is a receiving which is a kind of giving.*
>
> W.H.

This book is based on the principle that it is 'more blessed to give than to receive' and that success is found through giving. But there may be a twist in the tale, another angle to take into account.

Sometimes we 'give something' to people when we let them give something to us; the best way to help someone may be to ask them to help and if we refuse to accept such service we may in fact do a disservice. There are some people who are so fiercely independent that they don't like to accept help. They are proud of the fact that they can help other people but they don't need anyone to help them, thank you very much. But they may be at fault. Sometimes, receiving may be blessed as well as giving.

Illustrations abound. If a small child asks to help Mummy with the cooking it may not be of much practical assistance. In fact, it may slow the work down considerably. Yet it may be good to accept the 'help' in order that the child may develop new skills. How else can one learn?

In a family it is possible for parents to do too much for their children instead of allowing and encouraging those children to make their own contribution to family life. Wise parents not only know how to give but how to receive. And the same principle may pertain to other situations.

Retirement can be full of surprises! Among my retirement activities I have included the giving of religious instruction to a couple of classes of ten-year-olds in a government school. The kids have taught me a lot! At Christmas time they have designed greeting cards which have been among the most appreciated I have received. It is true that while some of the cards have been quite artistic, even ingenious, others have been rather poorly drawn. Yet the thought behind the cards has made them meaningful for me and for the children and I have not only been glad to receive them but also to express my genuine appreciation.

The outpouring of affection for the late Diana, Princess of Wales has been phenomenal and, like others, I have found it hard to analyse. But watching clips of her life I have observed that she was not only good at giving but at receiving. Children who presented posies were made to feel that their offerings really meant something and that, as a result, they could stand a few centimetres taller.

A Kind of Giving

If further personal illustrations may be permitted, I have spent many years in a helping profession and can recall numerous times when it has been more blessed to receive than to give because in a sense the receiving has been a kind of giving.

I recall a family I tried to help when I was a young man. Some might have described them as feckless. Certainly, their situation was rough and ready. In fact, the home was dirty and smelt in a way that is still pungent in my memory! I used to visit that home and it was a sign that I was getting somewhere when I was offered a cup of tea.

The cup usually looked rather grubby or greasy but in that situation to have refused to accept what was offered would have been regarded as an affront and would have set back what I was trying to do. And so the cup was received (in my left hand, in the hope of perhaps avoiding the worst of the germs?) and the bond of acceptance was strengthened.

Many years later in London, England, I had a part in organising a Christmas Day lunch and entertainment for hundreds of lonely folk and also in the distribution of carrier bags of 'goodies' to people sleeping out in the centre of the city. Many people wanted to help with this activity and that was fine.

I recall a woman doctor – an ear, nose and throat specialist, actually – who would come and wash dishes for most of Christmas Day. Then there was a well-to-do property developer eager to be up half the night distributing the carrier bags. I discovered that some, although not all, of those who offered help really needed help themselves even if not of a financial kind. Sometimes they had their own problems and loneliness was usually among them. It was important to accept offers of help – even beyond what were sometimes needed – because helping might be helpful for the helpers!

The great and good Albert Schweitzer – with doctorates in philosophy, theology, music and medicine – went to Africa to open a hospital at Lambaréné. He was actually erecting the building with his own hands when he saw one of the local native men squatting and watching. He asked the man to help but he refused saying that he could not do such work as he was an intellectual! But then and thereafter Schweitzer was wise enough to ask people to help him and, incidentally, help themselves in the process.

I have said elsewhere in this book that there are right and wrong ways of giving. In a sense, giving is an art to be developed. But the same could be said about taking. Help can be received with grace and appreciation so that its value is invested with added significance. Help well received can encourage further helpfulness to other people.

Something else, when we are ready to accept help we affirm the self respect of the other person and their realisation that they have something to contribute. As I have noted elsewhere, there are ways of giving that can make people feel put down. Being willing to accept their help can give them a lift and that can bring lasting good.

~ 26 ~

Give Yourself A Talking To

> *Self reverence, self knowledge, self control — these three alone lead life to sovereign power.*
>
> Tennyson

*I*t used to be said that talking to oneself was the first sign of insanity, but that's crazy and most of us do it anyway – even if our 'talking' is not audible. (Just watch the moving lips of people as they sit alone in their cars waiting for traffic lights to change!) What is more, there are plenty of examples of people for whom, far from signalling a flight from reason, talking to themselves has been the first sign of coming to their senses. Of course, everything depends on what we say in our 'self talk' but more of that in a moment...

This book is about giving and particularly about giving to others. However, unless we make adequate deposits in our own emotional and spiritual bank we will have precious little to give to others anyway. But giving ourselves 'a good talking to' may be a way of starting to top up our dwindling balances or at least stopping the seepage of resources.

I suspect that a lot of 'self-talk' doesn't help at all. It is negative and drains emotional reserves instead of building them up. For example, we rage because of a small scratch on the car and take no account of the fact that we have a house to live in and passable health with which we can enjoy many things. We give ourselves a hard time about the past which, while it can be forgiven, can never be altered. We get in a real lather with ourselves about future events which may never happen anyway. Some of the ways in which we rattle on to ourselves are enough to drive us crazy – well, almost! So we need to switch programs! Tuning in may take a little time but once we get into the habit of positive 'self talk' we will find it easy enough. As with most things, practice will make perfect.

Some may find it helpful to lock themselves in a quiet room or go for a walk in the country where they can talk to themselves, even audibly if desired, without fear of causing other people to raise their eyebrows. Some may find it even more helpful to write to themselves, taking care to keep the material private or to destroy it when it will no longer serve any useful purpose. The point is that articulating the pros and cons of anything may help us to clarify the issues instead of allowing them to go round and round in our minds for hour after hour like jumbled clothes in a spin drier.

Conversation Starters

What people should say to themselves is very much their own business, of course. Everyone's self dialogue will be different, but following are a few conversation starters which may be helpful, for some people at least.

For example, we might tell ourselves that it is important to *see the big picture* instead of an ant's eye view of the world. Viewed in the context of life as a whole, what troubles us may be a mere detail deserving of some attention but not something about which we should worry ourselves sick.

Then we might *catalogue some of the good things* we've got going for us. Sure, in our internal balance sheet there may be some debits, but what about the credits? What about the positive things? Do we live in a free country without fear of secret policemen knocking on our door in the dead of night? Do we have enough to eat? Do we have family and friends who care about us? Do we have reasonable health so that we can get about? If we can say yes to any or all of these questions we are more fortunate than many. And unless we are extremely thick we will be able to add many other items to our catalogue of benefits.

We might tell ourselves that we can only *live a day at time*. Our shoulders are not broad enough to carry the burdens of yesterday and the imagined crosses we may have to bear tomorrow as well as what must be borne today. The secret of living a day at a time is a strong point for members of Alcoholics Anonymous as they try to maintain sobriety but it could be a life-saver for a lot of other people as well. We should tell ourselves that – and often.

At times we may, in all honesty, *congratulate ourselves*. I have heard it said that "self praise is no recommendation". Certainly, we should have no time for boasting. But if we know that we have done first-class work or perhaps gone the extra mile in service there is nothing wrong in enjoying the satisfaction which is deserved. We may not get a rush of blood to the head but we can experience affirmation in our heart and feel grateful that we have been able to do some good. We might even arrange a little reward for ourselves. Why not?

On the other hand, there may be times when we should *take ourselves to task* for failing to live up to the standards we know are right and not try to fob ourselves off with any phoney alibis. After all, self deception is probably the worst deception of all and it really doesn't make much sense.

Very strongly, we should put it to ourselves that as the Almighty is willing to forgive us for our failures when he is asked, so we should be ready to *forgive ourselves*. It doesn't make sense to turn life into a never-ending guilt trip. The past cannot be re-lived but it can be out-lived!

We should remind ourselves of the cliché that today is the first day of the rest of our lives and that, if we can only believe it, the best is yet to be.

Our self talk may mostly consist of small talk but on a regular basis we should grant ourselves an interview with ourselves when we can get down to brass tacks, with some really straight talking about matters of the moment. And, without fail the interview should conclude with some systematic calling to mind of all those things for which we should be grateful. Self talk should finish on a high note rather than on a low one.

It was a Jewish songwriter who long ago talked to himself and was all the better for it. He said, "Bless the Lord, O my soul: and forget not all his benefits..." We might say much the same in our own words.

~ 27 ~

Give Training

> *To give training may be to open doors of opportunity.*
>
> W.H.

Athletes could scarcely be successful in their sports without diligent training. The giving and accepting of training is a prerequisite of success in many other activities as well. Everyone should gain all the skills they can, not only because they owe it to themselves but also so that they may be able to give the best possible service to other people.

For example, customers have every right to expect that salespeople will know their stuff, whether they are selling cars or cameras or whatever. Similarly, we expect our doctors to be up-to-date with regard to the latest drugs and treatments available. They may have graduated 30 years ago but we hope that they have kept themselves 'in training' so as to give us good treatment. The same could be said about almost any other form of service.

I have known situations where an organisation has devoted 60 per cent or 70 per cent of its expenditure to the payment of staff – including many professional people – but has been hard pressed to allocate much more than 1 per cent for in-service training. Yet in many fields it is important to stay abreast of rapid developments.

Knowledge doesn't stand still and we are never too young or too old to learn.

Valuable years may have been spent in colleges or other educational establishments. On-the-job experience (perhaps in apprenticeships) may have been equally important but even so, more input may be needed in a rapidly-changing scene. Modern technology has brought an information explosion which is both a boon and a challenge for us all. Peter Drucker has written, "Knowledge has to be improved, challenged and increased constantly or it vanishes."

Time was when people left school, went to a job and then continued in much the same kind of activity until retirement. Now that is happening less and less and training, retraining and then further retraining is required of more and more people. Some may find that tough, but it has to be. The wise will relish the thought of new learning curves and the challenges they bring.

Of course the amount of ongoing training required will be related to the kind of work involved, but employers owe it to themselves, their staff and their customers to ensure that people are equipped for the work they are expected to do. I have known situations where employees have received either no job descriptions, or some so scant as to be almost worthless, and little instruction. Then they have been denigrated for poor performance when perhaps it has been their employers who have been to blame.

So, the giving and receiving of training of one form or another may be important for us all. (Even successful retirement may call for a willingness to think new thoughts and learn new skills. To say that old dogs can't learn new tricks is a load of rubbish – if this 'old dog' may say so!)

Throwing Money

Organisations considering staff training should realise that while more expenditure may be necessary, throwing money at the idea may not be the only answer. The most expensive training experiences are not always the most valuable. Of the calling of conferences there seems to be no end and it is possible to go to seminar after seminar, which may be all very well. But the test is what happens after the seminars. Are the notes thrown into a cupboard and does the experience fade into oblivion? It can happen that way.

For that reason it is good if, having sent staff to a training experience, management arranges a follow-up interview and requires a report on what has transpired – even if securing it is like drawing teeth at times. The value of an experience which may have cost a great deal of time and money should not be allowed to evaporate. It is an investment that should bring a worthwhile return and that return needs to be monitored.

Sometimes valuable means of training may *not* be costly. In addition to keeping up with new developments it may be helpful for staff to tap into the corporate memory of their organisation. All wisdom was not born in this generation and those who went before were not all fools. Sometimes older members of staff or people newly retired can prove to be valuable mentors. In retirement I have taken part in a number of courses for rising executives from third world countries and hopefully those attending have been able to learn from my experience and especially from my mistakes!

Apprenticeships and training schemes which bring young people into close contact with skilled operators can be invaluable – especially when the instructors can inculcate work ethics as well as technical information.

In their training of staff some firms give big emphasis to small things – like greeting customers and seeking to understand their requirements. I visit supermarkets where those on the checkouts are invariably pleasant and helpful. No doubt, many of the staff are naturally inclined that way but I suspect that there has also been some schooling about the suitable response to customers. That is good, for the importance of little things should not be overlooked.

Then firms are wise to see employees as potential customers and to give encouragement with staff discounts. Apart from anything else, it certainly helps their pitch when salespeople can say that they have personally found a product helpful. That kind of testimony can make all the difference.

Leaders should know that if they build their people their people will build their business. We often speak about 'go-getters' and what they can achieve. But 'go-givers' may be even more significant. Some employees work for a wage – nothing more and nothing less. Some also work for a company. Others work for the customers. Perhaps the aim should be to train and equip people to work for all three and to seek triple win results. That sounds like a recipe for success.

~ 28 ~

Give A Reason

> *Be prepared to give...the reason for the hope you have.*
> The Bible: New International Version

When as a boy I was told to do something I sometimes had the temerity to ask "Why?" The answer I sometimes got was, "Because I say so" – which I never found entirely satisfactory. I have known bosses who have, in effect, given the same sort of response to their staff. They have cloaked their actions in secrecy and in dealing with employees have believed in "working them hard and telling them nothing" as one boss I knew used to say.

Now sometimes commercial confidentiality has to be maintained for very good reasons. At other times leaders may not feel free to lift the veil of someone else's privacy. In some cases a premature disclosure of plans could cause problems. Almost anyone who has been in management could cite such instances.

But when we can do so I believe that we should 'tell it like it is'. Giving people reasons for what they are asked to do is a way of showing respect for them as intelligent human beings and will help to ensure successful working relationships. If we don't provide explanations, someone else will imagine a reason for what is happening and spread it as though it was 'gospel truth'. The rumours could be damaging and almost certainly will be wide of the mark.

I once knew a dear fellow who seemed to thrive on secrecy. If some people were not confidential enough – a real problem at times – he took things to the extreme and would speak in hushed tones about the most inconsequential of matters.

One of the secrets of Field Marshall Lord Montgomery's success as a leader was that he was not remote or removed. He met the troops where they were and told them what he could, with the result that they felt that they were not merely 'cannon fodder' but colleagues with Monty in a great endeavour. Montgomery's personalised approach had a lot to do with the morale and success of his forces in the field.

I have sometimes met staff in groups of 30 or 40 and given them the opportunity to raise any matters they wished. By way of a preface, I have usually said that if I didn't know the answer to a question I would say so and try to get the answer to them as soon as possible. In the same way if, for some valid reason, I couldn't give a complete disclosure on an issue, at least not immediately, I would explain this. Almost invariably the situation was accepted. I don't know how much staff learnt from my answers in those sessions but I certainly learnt a lot from the questions! And I believe that because reasons for policies were given, this made some matters more acceptable even if not always welcome.

Leaders Have to Lead

Wherever possible consultation should take place and decisions should be made on the broadest possible base of knowledge. Managers have to manage and leaders have to lead but some inkling of the reason for what is happening will often help people to implement plans with better grace. Of course, the important thing is to build confidence between the leader and the led, the management and the staff. If each can trust the other success may be assured. If there is no such confidence then defeat may well stare them in the face.

The value of giving a reason for things whenever possible can apply in many other situations. For example, it can help customer relations. Why has there been a change in a particular product?

What has caused delay in delivery? Why has an item gone out of production? If there is a known reason then it should be disclosed. People like to know and shouldn't be fobbed off.

Success in medical practice may also be helped by 'openness'. If at one time medics were inclined to dispense their pills and potions with a knowing look and pursed lips, hopefully that time has gone. Most patients like to know what and why treatment is prescribed and want it explained in non-technical language, as far as possible.

Sometimes there may be need for discretion with respect to the amount of disclosure but generally the open approach is favoured nowadays and that is good. There is nothing worse than being given the impression that you are simply a collection of symptoms or another 'case' rather than a thinking, feeling, fearing human being. Things may be bad but being given some reasons for what is being done helps the patient to make some sense of what he or she has to undergo.

The need to give reasons may never be more necessary than when dealing with volunteers. One of my mentors told me that the ultimate test of leadership is what it can do with people who have the right of refusal. The regimental sergeant major on the barrack square can bark out his orders and men fall in – or else! The finer points in the art of leadership may not be called into play. But mobilising the hearts and wills of volunteers so that they feel within themselves that they must do what they are asked is another matter entirely. That may call for an understanding of reasons as well as the spark of conviction.

Having argued the need to give reasons I have to say that few explanations will satisfy everyone. However cogent the case put forward some will say, "Ah, but..." Few armies would march into battle if generals had to wait until every last reservation was overcome. Rational human beings are not always amenable to reason. That is because all have some 'hang ups', prejudices and predilections which they may not even understand themselves. However, to fail to give reasons for action wherever possible is to insult intelligence and prejudice chances of successful working together. Sometimes the best we can do is to give reasons in all honesty and hope that they will be accepted. Then we must move on.

~ 29 ~

Give Happiness

> *If I have faltered more or less*
> *in my great task of happiness...*
> *Lord, Thy most pointed pleasure take*
> *And stab my spirit broad awake.*
>
> R. L. Stevenson

*H*uman happiness may not be the supreme good but life would be bleak without it! In some ways happiness is a by-product. We find it when we are looking for something else. For example, we may be seeking to create something of beauty or do a good turn and suddenly happiness comes upon us. We are 'surprised by joy'.

In one sense happiness is something which we must generate within ourselves, but there may be other ways of thinking about it. Dr Samuel Johnson was a famous English writer, a many-sided character and a devout soul who wrote prayers and regularly attended St Clement Danes Church in the city of London. He wrote, "I would like to be ordained so that I could pronounce the Absolution and *make unhappy people happy*".

But can we make other people happy? We wish people "a happy birthday" or hope that newly-weds will "live happily ever after" but can we make our wishes come true? The answer must be, "Not entirely". Yet we can and do contribute to the happiness of others. It has been said that all who joy would win must share it, for "happiness was born a twin".

The ways in which people can bring happiness to others are many and varied. Here I can only mention a few. First, there is *good humour*. Richard Whately, one-time Archbishop of Dublin, said that "Happiness is no laughing matter" but I for one am glad for those who have added to the sum of human happiness through the gift of laughter.

Some people have a positive genius for making people laugh. We may recall Charlie Chaplin or the Marx brothers or other famous manufacturers of mirth. Or we may think of people within our own circle who can be counted on to bring a smile to people's faces.

I have a good Scottish friend called David who has a broad accent and an incredible sense of humour. He also has a speech problem but far from being inhibited by this, he turns it to good account by laughing at himself and getting others to laugh with him and not at him. In a crowded dining room if there are peals of laughter coming from people at a particular table you can be sure that it will be where David is. He has dedicated his life in a serious vocation but far from being a hindrance, his sense of humour has been a help to him in his work.

We may or may not possess a special sense of fun but if we can sometimes raise a smile we may do more good than we realise. I have known times when a little humour has helped to resolve a tense business situation. Then the grace of God has been in a good laugh for someone who has been ill. So, while we may extol more lofty virtues let no one despise humour.

A Thing of Beauty

Then we can give happiness through sharing *beauty*. John Keats declared that "A thing of beauty is a joy forever" and we may all do something to bring beauty into the lives of other people.

I sat in a restaurant and could not help overhearing the conversation at the next table. An elderly woman who, apparently, lived alone was telling her friend about how she managed to cope and the fact that she didn't know how she would live without the sound of the music which meant so much to her. For such a person a well-chosen tape would be like a gift from heaven, I imagine.

For someone else we might consider giving a volume of poetry, a piece of beautiful china or even a fragrant rose. In my book, to share beauty in any form is to achieve success in the endeavour to make this planet a little more livable.

Some are able to create beauty and it would easy to reel off the names of composers and poets and artists galore but I will keep my illustrations within the circle of people I know. One is a friend called John who has a wonderful way with words. He can say more in one short poem than some can manage in a whole tome. He claims that when I was an editor I nagged him into writing prayer-poems and in that case I am glad to plead guilty, for those he produced have brought happiness and challenge to thousands of people around the world.

My wife and I have a friend called Yvonne who, with palette and brush, can depict Australian scenery in such a way that you can almost smell the gum trees and feel the hot sun shining through the picture. Her paintings hang in all sorts of places and bring much pleasure to many people. We may or may not have such creative talents but with a modicum of wit and wisdom we can be successful in sharing beauty and giving happiness to other folk.

Then we can give happiness though *friendship*. Informality is a mark of the present generation so that a whipper-snapper you have never met before will greet you by your first name as though you were a long-lost cousin. So be it. But friendship goes beyond friendliness although it may begin with it. We may have many acquaintances but fewer friends. They represent something deep and abiding.

Socrates said:

> *All people have their different objects of ambition –*
> *horses, dogs, money, honour as the case may be, but*
> *for my part I would rather have a good friend than all*
> *these put together.*

A simple soul who was one of Socrates' friends was asked to name the boon in life for which he was most grateful. His reply was, "That being such as I am I have the friends I have".

Without doubt some have a special gift for friendship. My daughter had some lovely friends at school and now as mature women they are still friends who keep their relationships in good repair and bring each other much support and happiness. For some people, however, giving and receiving friendship doesn't come easily. So what's the secret?

To quote Ralph Waldo Emerson: "The only way to have a friend is to be a friend." And Dale Carnegie put it like this, "You can make more friends in two months by becoming interested in other people than you can in two years by trying to get other people interested in you." In this as in other things success comes through giving.

Sometimes the expression of true friendship will be tough rather than tender. For example, there must be many young people who would be happily alive today if their friends had urged them not to drive too fast or after drinking alcohol. The same could be said of those who, under peer pressure, have experimented with drugs. They may have needed friends of a kind who would have helped to save them from themselves. Sometimes, that may be what friends are for – and we all need them, whatever our age.

True friendship is not exploitative and should not be abused. But through it can come the discovery of mutual benefits of many kinds. In *The Handbook of Selling* Charles B. Ruth wrote, "There are many cases of people who have nothing to offer a prospect except friendship out-selling salesmen with everything to offer – except friendship". More than any products we may produce people may value something of ourselves – which is a high compliment to us.

It is in giving happiness that we are likely to find it. That truth is so simple that many overlook it.

~ 30 ~

Give Forgiveness

> *There must be no bitterness in the reconstructed world...we must try to forgive those who injured us.*
>
> Madam Chiang Kai-shek

*I*t may be a sign that forgiveness is either rare or remarkable that it makes headlines. Consider the following accounts all taken from the news media.

Reported in Australia was an interview on British TV with a woman who, after 12 years of marriage and four children, had an affair which began at a Christmas party. She went along with the proposal of her lover that they should hire a hit man to kill her husband for a thousand pounds. The hit man disappeared but the plot was discovered and the woman was charged for her part in it. However, the husband forgave his wife and pleaded with the judge on her behalf. As a result she was given 200 hours of community service instead of a gaol sentence of up to five years. The husband received his wife back and claimed to still love her.

In the Possil district of Glasgow, Scotland, 12-year-old James came face-to-face with the mother of the boy aged 13 he had admitted to killing with a knife in self-defence. For a moment they stared at each other – the boy startled and afraid; the mother overwhelmed with mixed emotions. Then the tension broke. The mother found that she had no bitterness left and she swept the boy into her arms.

She told him, "Don't be afraid of me. You are just a wee boy. I bear you no grudge." James put his arms around the woman and kept repeating, "I am sorry...I am sorry." James's mother came along and later the two women, strangers until then, had a cup of tea together. The bereaved woman said, "I feel much better after seeing Jim. At the beginning I was bitter against the boy who took my son's life. But he is so young. He is just a little boy and I forgive him".

A man who described himself as a clerk wrote to an education committee in Gloucestershire, England. He said that his wages were small and that his wife was suffering from an incurable disease. He continued:

> *For several months my daughter has been pleading for a new cardigan to replace a very old, much worn one...the other girls had been making fun of her but I felt that I could not afford one. One day last week she went into the post office. At a table just inside the door was a young woman with her bag open and a wallet just inside.*
>
> *What came over my girl I don't know. She took the wallet and made for the street but the young woman was quick too. She jumped up and followed her. Outside within a few yards was a policeman and my daughter stood still, petrified, expecting to be denounced.*
>
> *But the young woman walked quietly up to her and took the wallet from her and asked why she had tried to steal it. Crying, my little one explained. Then in a very sweet manner, she told her how wrong it was to steal. Afterwards she took my daughter to a shop and bought her a pretty new cardigan.*

The father said that he wanted to trace the young woman and express his thanks. He thought that her name was Jackie and that she might be a teacher because of books seen in her bag....

From such facts we might turn to fiction and from newspaper journalese to the immortal words of Shakespeare in *The Merchant of Venice*:

> *The quality of mercy is not strain'd,*
> *It droppeth as the gentle rain from heaven*
> *Upon the place beneath: it is twice bless'd;*
> *It blesses him that gives and him that takes...*
> > *Therefore, Jew,*
> *Though justice be thy plea, consider this,*
> *That in the course of justice none of us*
> *Should see salvation: we do pray for mercy,*
> *And that same prayer doth teach us all to render*
> *The deeds of mercy.*

It is sometimes imagined that success is a prize for the hard-nosed and stony-hearted but second thoughts would suggest otherwise. Without the 'quality of mercy' so-called 'success' may be as arid as a desert and may be belied by the reality of bitterness and tension arising out of failure to forgive.

A House With a View

A couple in Wales built a splendid house on a mountain. There were six bedrooms as well as fine living accommodation and facilities. The view from the house was glorious and local people commented on how magnificent everything was. In fact, the reality was different. The man and his wife couldn't get along with each other. There were hard feelings between them and so they lived apart, occupying different rooms in what seemed to be their dream house. We may wonder whether at times their dream was more like a nightmare, for just as if we break the law of gravity we can break our necks, so if we break the 'law' of forgiveness, our own spirits may be broken. Then what price 'success'?

Ideally, forgiveness is a two-way street with the forgiving spirit being met by penitence but even without such a response the showing of mercy can be a powerful influence for good.

In 1908 Gandhi was attacked and nearly murdered by a religious fanatic but was unwilling to prosecute his attacker or give evidence against him. On the day of the crime and when he was at death's door Gandhi summoned his ebbing strength to issue an appeal. He said:

> *This man did not know what he was doing. He thought that I was doing what was wrong. He has had his redress in the only manner he knows. I, therefore, request that no steps be taken against him. I believe in him. I will love him and win him by love.*

Given the ongoing futility of tit-for-tat violence in some parts of the world it could be that forgiveness would break the deadly chain reaction. Is there any other way?

To bring matters nearer to home, a development on our crowded roads is what is described as 'road rage'. There is no doubt that some people change their characters when they get behind the wheel of a car. In the home they may be gentle and in the office unfailingly courteous. But on the road it may be a different story. Rather than being 10 minutes late in this life they run the risk of being 30 years early in the next! They have an urge to compete at any cost and if anyone gets in their way their anger seems to know no bounds. The 'penny hasn't dropped' and they haven't realised that giving way may be a sign of strength, not weakness. Forgiving road trespassers may be for the good of all concerned.

Of course, forgiveness is more than the mere mouthing of words. I recall the easy catch-phrase, "I'll forgive you, thousands wouldn't"; it doesn't mean much, as a rule. Words can be cheap but 'showing mercy' may be costly. The German poet Heinrich Heine, whose verses were set to music by composers such as Schumann and Schubert, was taken to task by his gentle wife. "Ask God to forgive you" she said, only to be answered with bitter irony, "God will forgive me; it is his trade". Such a cheap jibe can only lead us to conclude that with regard to divine forgiveness the poet didn't have a clue.

Including Ourselves

The person some people find it most difficult to forgive is themselves. They have done something of which they are ashamed or pursued a course which they deeply regret. Because of what they have done they may have blown a relationship apart and putting it together again now seems impossible. As a result any 'successes' in life are clouded by dark memories. The answer is in not only being ready to accept forgiveness but in being willing to forgive themselves instead of remaining their own perpetual accusers.

When we are at peace with ourselves it is easier for us to be at peace with other people. Having found forgiveness we may then have the grace to forgive other people. Someone who did that was Pastor Billup in the Deep South of the United States of America. One night he was abducted by eight robed and hooded men of the Klu Klux Klan who tied him to a tree and chain whipped him.

Finally, and with derision no doubt, they invited him to pray. He did so, saying, "Father, forgive them for they do not know what they do". He didn't pray for his own safety but for his tormentors, their wives and families. He asked that they would not have to suffer for what they had done and – amazingly – the gang did not kill him outright but left him tied to the tree while they drove off.

Three years later at midnight Billup heard a knocking on his parsonage door. A young white man stood before him, obviously distressed and wanting to come into the house. He said, "Reverend, you don't know me but I know you. I am one of the eight men who beat you...I have been going crazy ever since and don't want to continue living this way." He blurted out the names of the other seven men and told Billup to phone the police, saying that he would be ready to witness to the truth in court as he couldn't stand keeping silent any longer.

Billup responded by telling the young man that he had no intention of calling the police and that they probably both needed forgiveness more than they needed the police. Then he prayed for forgiveness for them both, the young man left and Billup never saw him again.

A similar spirit was shown by the unknown writer of a prayer found in the notorious Ravensbruck concentration camp:

> *O Lord remember*
> *not only the men and women of goodwill,*
> *but also those of ill will.*
>
> *Do not remember*
> *all the suffering they have inflicted on us;*
> *remember the fruits we have bought*
> *thanks to this suffering –*
> *our comradeship, our loyalty,*
> *our humility, our courage,*
> *our generosity, the greatness of heart*
> *which has grown out of all this,*
> *and when they come to judgement*
> *let all the fruits*
> *that they have borne be their forgiveness.*

~ 31 ~

Give A Positive Expression

> *Attitudes are more important than facts.*
> Karl Menninger

*I*n her book *The Idea Factory* Valerie Parv wrote about a Dr Dennis Waitley who was asked to help a retail store solve the problem of a rise in shoplifting. He arranged to have words set to music and broadcast. The message was "Don't shoplift, don't shoplift" but the problem actually increased because the ditty gave unconscious minds the wrong message and planted an unfortunate idea in people's thoughts. People didn't absorb the 'don't' part of the message but only the 'shop-lift' part and tended to act accordingly. When the message was changed to, "Please pay at the door" things began to improve!

We often spend more time saying what we *don't* want people to do than what we *do* expect from them. I read a magazine put out from a seniors' complex during the absence on holiday of the very positive-minded manager. The pages were peppered with 'don'ts'. Any minor misdemeanour by one hapless individual brought an admonition for the hundreds of residents who would read the magazine. If only directions could have been couched in positive terms how much more acceptable and effective they would have been!

A poster in a nursing home may have summed up the feelings of many people. It read, "Don't tell me what I'm doing wrong, tell me what I'm doing right." In fact, with a little thought it is possible to address even negative behaviour in a positive way – and get better results.

The messages we give within the family setting are also better if put in positive form. Instead of saying, "Don't forget to buy the milk" we may say, "Remember to buy the milk". That way our subconscious mind may be more likely to 'remember to remember' instead of 'remembering to forget'. Even in the messages we give to ourselves, the positive form is likely to be more effective. Instead of telling ourselves, "Don't forget to telephone your mother" we may tell ourselves to *remember* to do it, with confidence that is what we will do.

In Negative Mode?

It will be difficult for us to give a positive expression to other people if our minds are set in a negative mode. Even if we use the right form of words our faces and our body language will be liable to give us away. One of President Lincoln's colleagues suggested a candidate for the cabinet. Lincoln refused the proposal saying, "I don't like the man's face". "But sir, he can't be responsible for his face", said the adviser. "Every man over forty is responsible for his face", replied Lincoln.

Having put down that quotation I felt like rushing to a mirror, fearing the worst! Then I recalled a long-forgotten bit of doggerel: "My face I don't mind it for I am behind it but the people in front feel the jar!"

Before we can effectively give positive expression we need to tap into what Dr Norman Vincent Peale called 'the power of positive thinking', but for some temperaments that is not easy. It is said that 'a pessimist feels bad when he's good and fears it will be worse if he gets better'. In one of her Christmas Day broadcasts Queen Elizabeth said, "The optimist proclaims that we live in the best of all possible worlds. The pessimist fears that it is true."

Some sanguine temperaments always tend to see things in the best light while others may be more aware of the problems. Some find it hard to trust anyone, including themselves. One such character said, "When it comes to believing in myself, I'm an agnostic." If some folk don't actually write themselves off they constantly put themselves down so that they are demoralised and less than fully effective. They see a difficulty in every possibility instead of seeing a possibility in every difficulty. They are not defeated by problems but by lack of faith in themselves.

In *Ordering Your Private World* Gordon MacDonald wrote about what he called the 'sink-hole syndrome'. (A sink hole is a funnel-shaped depression where ground water or a spring has caused an underground cavity in limestone. The spring may dry up but the earth over it can cave in so that even cars and houses have been known to disappear.) Perhaps a kind of emptiness deep within us can cause an emotional 'sink hole' to open up.

But I believe that even if we are prone to become depressed and are pessimists by nature we can become optimists by grace. We need not stay the way we are. While some may have profound psychological problems requiring specialist treatment, for the majority pessimism need not be an incurable 'disease' and self-treatment may be all that is required.

We can talk ourselves into a better frame of mind. Henry David Thoreau, the American writer, naturalist and philosopher would, on waking, lie in bed for a while telling himself all the good news he could remember and then rise to meet the day in a world filled with good things, fine people and great opportunities.

We can saturate our thinking with positive ideas from motivational books or tapes. Personally, I have found it helpful to drop positive seed thoughts from the Bible into my mind, particularly when I have been worried. Examples (from the New International Version) might be, "The Lord is my Shepherd, I shall lack nothing" (Psalm 23: 1) or, "You will keep in perfect peace him whose mind is steadfast, because he trusts in you" (Isaiah 26: 3). There are many other helpful quotations where those came from or, for some, inspiration may be derived from other sources.

The process may take time – a lifetime even – but we can with confidence expect improvement. We can condition our minds to think health and success and peace, and as we think so we are likely to be. Prospects can appear brighter and our zest for living can increase and as it does so we will be able to give a positive expression to others.

I came across a number of statements by an unnamed author under the title, *Winning Ways*. I quote a few of them as follows:

> *A winner goes through a problem; a loser goes around it, and never gets past it.*
>
> *A winner knows what to fight for, and what to compromise on; a loser compromises on what he shouldn't and fights for what isn't worthwhile fighting about.*
>
> *A winner says, "I'm good, but not as good as I ought to be"; a loser says "I'm not as bad as a lot of other people".*
>
> *A winner explains; a loser explains away. A winner feels responsible for more than his job; a loser says, "I only work here". A winner says, "There ought to be a better way to do it"; a loser says, "That's the way it's always been done here".*

Would-be Winners

As would-be winners we can give positive expressions to others and contribute to success for all concerned. We can do it through what Robert Schuller calls *'possibility thinking'*. Other people may have looked at a problem for so long that they can no longer see it clearly. With fresh eyes we may see it in a new light and be able to give some positive suggestions.

Leslie Weatherhead wrote about a picture in which the artist had sought to depict an interview between Faust and Satan. Faust had gambled for his soul and the artist depicted the two sitting at a chess board, Satan on one side and Faust on the other. In the painting the Devil was gloating because he thought he had Faust completely beaten. It certainly looked like checkmate. However, one day a master chess player studied the painting and then, to the surprise of everyone in the art gallery, shouted, "It's a lie! The king and the knight *can* move!"

Someone able to see possibilities can be a life-saver for people in all kinds of situations. For example, I have known people who have been distracted through looking in vain for work or frustrated by the dead-end job which they have had. They have not known which way to turn until someone has been able to suggest a career change or a business opportunity which has made all the difference. If in this or in other ways we can help someone else, it will bring us the enormous satisfaction of shared success.

Then we may give a positive expression through *encouragement*. There are plenty of people who are experts at giving discouragement. The 'cold water treatment' is one of their specialities. But 'encouragers' are rare spirits and the world owes them more than may be realised.

Many years ago a young man wanted to be a writer but his prospects were poor. For one thing, he had only had four years schooling. His father had gone to prison for not paying his debts and the hungry young man was reduced to pasting labels on bottles in a rat-infested warehouse and sleeping at night in a dismal attic with two other poor boys.

Nothing daunted, he submitted story after story without success. Then one was accepted and an editor praised him. That was the turning point and Charles Dickens never looked back. The name of the editor may be forgotten but the fruit of his encouragement remains.

Clifton James was Field Marshal Montgomery's official 'double' during the Second World War and was studying Montgomery during a rehearsal for D-Day. He wrote:

> *Within a few yards of where I was standing a very young soldier, still looking seasick from his voyage, came struggling along gamely trying to keep up with his comrades in front. I could imagine that, feeling as he did, his rifle and equipment must have been like a*

ton weight. His heavy boots dragged in the sand, but I could see that he was fighting hard to conceal his distress. Just as he got level with us he tripped up and fell flat on his face.

Half sobbing he heaved himself up and began to march off 'dazedly' in the wrong direction. Monty went straight up to him and with a quick, friendly smile turned him round. 'This way, sonny. You're doing well – very well. But don't lose touch with the chap in front of you.' When the youngster realised who it was who had given him friendly help his expression of dumb admiration was a study.

Montgomery's combination of discipline and encouragement made a private in his army feel worth a colonel in any other!

One way in which we may encourage people is by 'setting them up' for small successes and gradually raising the bar and increasing the challenges as their confidence grows. If we can convey to people that we believe in them it may help them to believe in themselves and set them on the way to achievement. Our gift of encouragement may be worth more than a million dollars to someone.

If we have a strong personal *faith* that may also be a strong resource for other people. We may or may not trumpet our belief but folk will get the message, if not only through what we say then through what we are. They will realise that we have 'invisible means of support'.

I have a friend who has been fighting a deadly disease for a long time. I have lost count of the number of operations he has undergone and can only imagine what discomfort he has endured. Yet he remains unfailingly positive and cheerful. He is not a preacher man but without him saying much the message has come through – loud and clear: his fortitude is derived from his faith and no expression could be more positive.

If we can give a positive expression in a world which may often seem to be filled with negatives our contribution to others will be enormous.

~ 32 ~

Final Focus

> *Teach us...to give and not to count the cost.*
>
> Ignatius Loyola

When my brother and I were boys we would sometimes burn messages on spare pieces of card by means of a magnifying glass and pin-point focusing of the rays of the sun. It took patience, particularly in Britain where sunshine was often less plentiful than in some other places! But we felt that it was worthwhile, for all that.

It would be my hope that with the diffused light from material in this book readers may be able to pin-point and focus the message for them in such a way that it may be burnt into their memory. In essence, the message is that only as we learn to give do we learn to live. In what sometimes seems to be a 'smash-and-grab' world that may not be the popular view, but wisdom ancient and modern would confirm that it is the right one.

In a general sense most people would agree that giving is a good thing. Fine! But what can we do to focus that assent in a way that will make a mark? For some the answer may be in voluntary service or in new approaches to their working life. It may find expression in giving to worthy charities or in seeking to improve personal relationships. As I have written this book I have been challenged myself. Hopefully, the same will have been true for some who have read it.

Deliberately, this book is not religious in a narrow or sectarian sense. My hope would be that its core idea may find acceptance across a wide spectrum of belief and unbelief. It will have been apparent that personally I have a strong Christian faith but also that I respect and reach out to those who do not.

Many have found that there is joy in giving as well as in getting, and success of many kinds attends those who set out to help others help themselves. May this book be a help to the helpers!

Also by
Wesley Harris
and available from Wrightbooks

NICE GUYS CAN WIN!
ISBN: 1875857 12 5

There are many examples of people who achieve apparent success by devious methods. Wesley Harris does not deny that *some* bad guys do win in certain ways. He also does know of very many people, from all walks of life, who are considerate to others, fair-minded, have high moral standards and yet are undoubtedly successful both in business and in life. In this book he shows, not only that good guys *can* win, but that very many *do*.

YOU'VE GOT WHAT IT TAKES
ISBN: 1875857 34 6

Many 'ordinary' people have performed extraordinary feats when the situation demanded. In a crisis they found reserves of strength they did not know they possessed, they performed above themselves. And, probably, so would we if the situation arose. But for most of us the

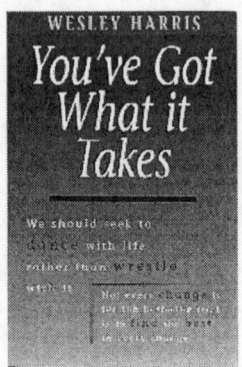

situation does not arise and so we never need to draw on our
reserves – indeed, we don't even know we have them! This book
is a guide to exploring such ability, talent and potential for
success.

TRUTH – STRANGER THAN FICTION

ISBN: 1875857 53 2

If this were a work of fiction some of the
stories would probably be described as
"too far-fetched" or "things which just
don't happen in real life." And yet these
stories are about real life, every one is
absolutely authentic – indeed, the author
has gone to considerable lengths to verify
them. Of course, it would be easy for the cynic to dismiss the
events described in these pages simply as a succession of
coincidences. On the other hand, the believer would be in no doubt
that they were a result of divine intervention. Wesley Harris
invites his readers to judge these stories for themselves.